THE PLEASURE OF THINKING

A JOURNEY THROUGH THE SIDEWAYS LEAPS OF IDEAS

Theodore Dalrymple

GIBSON SQUARE

Also by Theodore Dalrymple:

Spoilt Rotten
Litter: the Remains of Our Culture

Theodore Dalrymple currently gives expert psychiatric assessments in murder trials. Previously he worked as a doctor in Africa and the Gilbert Islands. Upon his return to England, he worked as a psychiatrist and GP in a prison hospital in the Midlands, and the East End of London. He is a regular contributor to, among others, The Times, Telegraph and the British Medical Journal.

First published in 2012 by Gibson Square Books

www.gibsonsquare.com

ISBN: 978-1-908096-08-1

Printed and bound by CPI Group (UK) Ltd, Croydon, CR0 4YY

The Pleasure of
Thinking

To Mr Stephen Wycherley,
who has sold me books for more than thirty years,
this book is dedicated.

Contents

'The miseries of a vacant life were never known to a man whose hours were insufficient for the inexhaustible pleasures of study.'
Edward Gibbon, *Memoirs of My Life and Writings*

'When we read, we thereby save ourselves the greater part of the trouble of thinking. This explains our obvious sense of relief when we turn from our own thoughts to reading.'
Arthur Schopenhauer, *Parerga et Paralipomena*

'The bibliomania, or the collecting an enormous heap of books without intelligent curiosity, has, since libraries have existed, infected weak minds, who imagine that they themselves acquire knowledge when they keep it on their shelves. Their motley libraries have been called the madhouses of the human mind...'
Isaac d'Israeli, *Curiosities of Literature*

'Brown varnished bookshelves lined the walls, filled with row upon row of those thick, heavy theological works which the second-hand booksellers generally sell by weight.'
Aldous Huxley, *Crome Yellow*

Small Beginnings

Not long ago in Manchester, I entered a small bookshop with a few second-hand books. I picked up a slim volume with the less-than-enthralling title, *Making Sense of the NHS Complaints and Disciplinary Procedures*, published in a series called *The Business Side of General Practice*. I cannot now recall what induced me to pick up such a volume, but I was soon glad that I did.

In the foreword, Sir Donald Irvine, the then-president of the General Medical Council, the disciplinary body that supervises the medical profession in Great Britain, wrote:

> Patients today are seeking better protection
> from poorly performing doctors...

Inside the book was a slip of paper from the Small Practices Association, asking for a review of the book for its professional journal.

The reviewer asked was Dr Harold Shipman, and his review was due six months before he was arrested for having murdered many patients.

I know from the greying of the edges of such a book when it has been read from cover to cover, and this book had been read in such a fashion. It is unlikely that anyone other than Dr Shipman had ever read it.

I bought it for five pounds, with Somerset Maugham's question to those who think they are superior because they read incessantly, from the beginning of his short story, *The Book-Bag*, ringing in my mind's ear:

> From the standpoint of what eternity is it better to have read a thousand books than to have ploughed a thousand furrows?

In 1794 Xavier de Maistre, younger brother of Joseph, the great reactionary philosopher, published his *Voyage autour de ma chambre*, Journey Round my Bedroom. In it he said:

> When I travel through my room, I rarely follow a straight line: I go from the table towards a picture hanging in a corner; from there, I set out obliquely towards the door; but even though, when I begin, it really is my intention to go there, if I happen to meet my armchair en route, I don't think twice about it, and settle down in it without further ado.

The journey towards the door continues...

1

Suburban Son

My copy of Somerset Maugham's first book, *Liza of Lambeth*, has the small and neat inscription, 'E.S. Labouchère', in it. Labouchère is not a common name and I suppose – or rather I like to suppose – that E.S. was some relative of Henry, the liberal politician and journalist.

The latter, born to immense wealth, ran up debts to £6000 (equivalent today of perhaps £500,000) while a student at Cambridge. An idler and a gambler in his early life, his family got him accepted in the Foreign Office without his knowledge. Offered the Second Secretaryship at the embassy in Buenos Aires while he was playing roulette at Baden Baden at about the same time as Dostoyevsky, he replied that he would accept the job on one condition only: that he could fulfil his duties from Baden Baden.

Henry Labouchère owes such undying fame in literary history as he possesses to something uncharacteristic of him. Although a radical liberal in politics, anti-imperialist and favourably disposed to Irish nationalism, as well as unconventional in his private life, it was he, as a Liberal MP, who introduced and argued for the clause in the Criminal Justice Amendment Act of 1885 under which Oscar Wilde was prosecuted in the following decade.

What E.S. thought of all this I cannot say, of course. The copy of *Liza of Lambeth* is a second, not a first edition, but published in the same year as the first, 1897, when Maugham was still a medical student. I came across it for sale for two pounds in a small bookshop run in what is now euphemistically called an inner city. (Frankness and plain speaking about things formerly taboo, it seems, is always accompanied by the erection of new taboos elsewhere.)

The shop was owned and run by a communist of the Enver Hoxha faction, a member of a small but select band of harmless fanatics. Albania was his Valhalla. He ran the shop half as a business and half as a missionary enterprise to the local population, whom he hoped to convert to the Albanian road to socialism. He had a technical vocabulary which was especially rich in terms of abuse, but not vulgar abuse.

For example, anyone associated with or supporting the Labour Party was 'a Labourite.' The scorn with which he managed to imbue this word, without however any excess of emphasis, was quite something to experience, and was a triumph of intonatory implication. He hated the Labourites (indeed anyone whose appellation ended in the suffix 'ites,' for example the Titoites and the Khrushchevites) much more than the Tories. The latter were good old-fashioned class enemies, whom one could respect or even pity in a way, for they were on the losing side of history, but the Labourites were class traitors, much worse than mere enemies. They confused the potentially revolutionary proletariat with ideas of reform, to say nothing of bread and circuses. The local council being in the control of the Labourites, he was always in dispute with it.

It was a matter of deep regret to him that it was a member of the relatively moneyed middle classes – in short, I – who was much his best customer. Indeed, as far as I could tell his stock scarcely varied – until, that is, it grew smaller by of my purchases.

The local population was not very literary in its pursuits. He would have been hard put to find a less auspicious place, the low rent notwithstanding, for a second-hand bookshop. The passing trade was all but nil, and he refused, on ideological grounds, to advertise. On the other hand, the lack of interest did make him relatively immune to shoplifting and burglary. He could put books outside on a shelf outside his shop and no one would take them. He would probably have had to pay people to do so.

An even bitterer disappointment to him was the uninterest of the local ethnic people – the area was multicultural, to use another current euphemism – in books, apart from the odd ganja-smoking Rastafarian revolutionary intellectual whom he would try to dissuade, I suspect without much success, from using mind-and-logic-destroying drugs. Elderly black women of the church-going persuasion would sometimes come in but, although all the available wall-space was covered in original propaganda posters from the Irish War of Independence, and of Mao on the Long March (in the days before he betrayed the working class in general, and Enver Hoxha in particular), the women were always interested in cheap bibles or in studies of the extremer prophets of the Old Testament. They were women who on Sunday wore white gloves and spoke in tongues.

The owner always lamented after they had departed the shop that it was a great pity that they suffered from the absurd kind of false-consciousness (religion) that was a baleful mental hangover from slavery. He wanted to alert them to their own true, that is to say material, interests, but it did not work. Haranguing them had no effect, so he attempted to awaken political outrage in them by means of reprints of a work of the Rev. Edward Blyden, *Christianity, Islam and the Negro Race*, first published in 1888. The Rev. Blyden he regarded as lying halfway between the ridiculous pastors of the local pentecostal churches and Enver Hoxha, and therefore as a step in the right direction for those who were utterly blinded.

I might be wrong, but I think I was the only person ever to have bought a copy of the Blyden reprint from him. He had a first edition, but he wouldn't sell it to me. I was interested in Blyden because I had once written a book about Liberia, now to be found in Oxfam bookshops at very low prices, even, or especially, when signed, and Blyden was a very important figure in Liberian history. Once you have written a book about a subject you remain interested in it no matter how obscure it might appear to the average man.

Blyden was born in what were still, then, the Danish West Indies, and later went to the United States, where he found so much prejudice against him that he emigrated to the newly-independent republic of Liberia. He learnt Latin, Greek and Hebrew, and was appointed professor of Greek at Liberia College; when he came to England, he was introduced to such luminaries as W.E. Gladstone and Thomas Hodgkin, the first describer of Hodgkin's disease. I happened to have a copy of an earlier book of Blyden's, *Liberia's Offering*, published in 1862, a collection of essays and sermons, including *A Vindication of the African Race; Being a Brief Examination of the Arguments in Favor of African Inferiority*.

But no amount of begging would persuade the bookseller to part with his copy, which he kept in a special closed bookcase. No, he said, he wanted to keep it to show his black customers that blacks had acceded to literary civilisation more than a century ago, and that they had nothing to be ashamed of. Indeed, their rightful place was in the vanguard of the coming cultural and political revolution.

With the women, however, he had to admit defeat. Nothing he said could deflect them from their false consciousness. He pointed them to the bible and theology shelves, and also to his surprisingly large section on spiritualism, in which there were probably upwards of three hundred books.

Spiritualism, it turned out, was also not their thing. They spoke with the voice of prophets, not with the voice of the dead. Spiritualism was white, not black.

But why did a dialectical materialist have so many books on so immaterial a subject? I asked him, and he told me that he had bought the entire personal library of a spiritualist who had died. Every habitué of English second-hand bookshops knows the orange-coloured limp wrappers of the *Left Book Club*, published in the 1930s by Victor Gollancz, denouncing the Fascists, supporting the Communists, warning against Hitler, fulminating against unemployment, publishing Arthur Koestler, George Orwell and Stephen Spender; such will recognise also the grey cloth covers of the *Right Book Club*, set up in unsuccessful opposition to the Left, denouncing the spread of communism, atheism and anticlericalism, and publishing Evelyn Waugh. But very few, I suspect, will know of the existence at the same time of the *Psychic Book Club*. Certainly I did not until I frequented this shop, whose spiritualist section, incidentally, was overlooked by a colour lithograph portrait of Stalin.

The Psychic Book Club published hundreds of titles, all in uniform blue cards. The collection had belonged to W. Bristow, who inscribed his name and address on the inside cover of each in the spidery hand with smudges that often resulted from the use of an old steel nib dipped in an inkwell. W. Bristow's hand, I surmised, was that of a clerk, a respectable man whose spiritualism was a kind of guilty secret.

And indeed, when out of idle curiosity I went to the address it was in a road redolent of past respectability, small Victorian terraced houses with disintegrating touches of mass-produced Venetiana and names like Crimea Terrace. The respectability had gone, of course, to be replaced by the mass bohemianism of our times, all cannabis and rock music. But it was not difficult to imagine the days when net curtains twitched as neighbours acted as the secret police of respectability, watching all the comings and goings in the road.

In my youth I would have sneered at the absurdity of spiritualism, but the passage of time increases one's tolerance of the harmless errors of others, and the awareness that one's own life has not exactly been a model of error-free rationality, but rather the reverse (as all human lives are), that is to say one of irreversible mistakes, renders one more forgiving. It takes no great effort of the imagination to understand the sorrows – the very sorrows that, sooner or later, are incident upon human life itself – to which spiritualism is a response. It is not that truth becomes relative, but rather that the importance of truth in human existence does so.

I bought just a few of W. Bristow's books, among them

one written in two volumes by a surgeon, with the title (perhaps not altogether encouragingly for his patients) *Thirty Years
among the Dead*. He is not speaking here of the post-mortem
room, however, but of the hereafter, which he explored with
great thoroughness, or at least pedantry. Another book I
bought was *Parish the Healer* by Maurice Barbanell, author also
of *The Trumpet Shall Sound* and *They Shall Be Comforted*. In the
rear of the book other volumes in the series are advertised: *On
the Edge of the Etheric* (40,000 copies sold), for example, and
*Materialisations and the Case of Clive-Holmes: The Laws behind
Psychic Phenomena and a Medium's Martyrdom*.

W. Bristow came into possession of *Parish the Healer* in
April, 1938. There is a frontispiece portrait of the subject
from a painting by Marcel Pontin. W.T. Parish, a distin-
guished-looking man of about sixty, stares three-quarter face
into the distance of infinity, his eyes evidently of that aqua-
marine clarity that is always disconcerting. He is firm in his
expression, but kindly in an abstract way: his kindliness is ideological rather than a spontaneous and warm response to an
individual human being before him.

There is a mixed visual metaphor in the painting. Hovering
behind the strongly-painted figure of Parish is a rather ghost-
ly or ectoplasmic Christ with hooded eyes, as if he is suffering from a mild case of *myasthenia gravis*. But Parish, incon-
gruously, is wearing a white coat, just like that of a hospital
doctor or a laboratory scientist. It seems that the authority of
both religion and science is being claimed here; but of course,
wanting the best of both worlds is human, all too human.

W.T. Parish, we learn, was a senior employee of a railway
company when he discovered his spiritual powers of healing,
his first patient being his wife. His fame grew, and his flat

became a real centre of such healing. He received there fifteen thousand letters a year from all over the world. His flat was in East Sheen.

When I read that, I confess that I laughed. I was reminded of a patient of mine who thought – in fact, knew – that he was Christ.

'How do you know?' I asked.

'My father, who art in Heaven, hath told me.'

'And your mother?'

'Oh, she lives in South Shields.'

It is not easy to say exactly why East Sheen and South Shields should be disqualified from being either spiritual centres or the domicile of the mother of God. But the idea that they might be nevertheless seems preposterous. After all, spirituality by definition is not less spiritual by being exercised in one place rather than another, and God's preference for the poor (to say nothing of sinners) could very well be expressed by having the Mother of God live in South Shields.

When I bought these books, I was anxious to make it clear to the bookseller that I did not do so because I was myself in regular contact with the dead. (Incidentally, the word dead in *Parish the Healer* is always placed in inverted commas, as 'dead,' rather as the word civilization is now always placed inverted commas in books by modern politically-correct scholars in the humanities. Who says that 'civilization' is 'dead?') I told him that I was buying them out of psychological interest.

But why was I so eager to dissociate myself in his mind from spiritualism? Though his views were freakish, I did not want him to think I was a freak for, strange to relate, we were agreed on many matters.

We were, of course, strongly divided by our opinions of Albania to which, unlike him, I had actually travelled during what I suppose he would have called the good old days. There I saw the horrors of communist totalitarianism at their most extreme (apart from North Korea, with perhaps the last days of Ceausescu vying and tying for the honour of second place). Such was my detestation of these regimes that a man who could hold up any one of them as a model for all mankind to imitate should have been beyond the pale for me.

Perhaps I was sensitised to the horrors of communism by the fact that my father was a communist (in opinion, if not in conduct); and there were many things about him and his character from which I wished to distinguish myself, from his opinions to his character. It is easier to change one's opinions than one's character. (Unfortunately, a wish to distinguish oneself from someone, especially a parent, often discloses a secret fear or awareness that one's wish is a manifestation of similarity, not of difference. So it was and is with my father and me: and the moment that I let my guard down, the moment that I lose my self-control, I am he.)

Perhaps, then, it is not so surprising that, despite my genuine and utter detestation of what the bookseller loved and believed should be the whole end of human existence, and for the horrible means by which he though that this should be brought about, I should also have had much in common with him. There are some people, I know, who cannot tolerate the sight or company of those of very different political, religious or philosophical opinions from themselves, but this, it seems to me, is to cut oneself off from too large a portion of

humanity. If poetic faith requires the willing suspension of
disbelief, civilised living requires the willing disregard of disagreement. 'As long as an act remains in bare intention alone,'
said the great eighteenth-century judge, Lord Mansfield, 'it is
not punishable by our law.' So long as a man does not put his
vile thoughts into action, he should not be excluded from our
human sympathies: let him who is without vile thoughts con-
sort only among the similarly pure-minded. God knows what
they would talk about.

And so I loved to discuss with him – perhaps lament
would be a better word – the cultural degeneration and decadence that we both saw all about us. No one read anything any
more, popular culture was nothing but a sink of vulgarity and
stupidity etc., etc., etc.

My Albanianite, who saw this vulgarity and decadence all
as the last gasp of a chronically-dying capitalism, could have
been a retired admiral writing letters of disgust to the newspapers from deepest Tunbridge Wells. He was a pure Luddite
where electronic apparatus was concerned (I had to pretend
to him that I had a mobile telephone only so that the hospital
or my patients might reach me, and that I never used it for
making bookings at restaurants). He thought the internet was
an instrument designed by the central committee of the bour-
geoisie to stupefy the masses and turn them away from the
works of Enver Hoxha – upon which they would otherwise
be engaged. He therefore refused absolutely to look up the
value of his stock on the internet, believing in any case that
books, like everything else, should be priced according to their
use-value, rather than their rarity-value. Very occasionally he
would look something up in old green-covered volumes called
Book Sales, but as these dated from the 1970s, his researches

tended to favour the customer rather than himself.

And so it was that I bought a second edition of *Liza of Lambeth* for two pounds. Though I warned him that it (and many similar purchases) were worth more, he was a man of honour. If he had marked it at two pounds, that was the price at which he would sell it.

2

Artful Sincerity

One finds things in old books: principally mummified insects of course, but also bloodstains, pressed flowers, old bus tickets, shopping lists, shipping manifests, builders' estimates for repairs to be done, butchers' bills, bookmarks that advertise life insurance, arts festivals and bookshops, and some even call the reader to faith and repentance (for example, 'Ho, everyone that thirsteth, come ye to the waters, and he that hath no money; come ye, buy and eat...,' which some these days would take more as an invitation to shoplifting in the name of social justice.) Many old books come from the houses of inveterate smokers; whenever, for example, I open my copy of Father Copleston's book about Nietzsche, I feel like a Lilliputian suddenly dropped into a Brobdingnagian ashtray, so powerful is the smell of stale – very, very stale – tobacco.

Of all the objects found in books, however, perhaps the most interesting, the most stimulating to the imagination, are letters. In a copy of *Underground Russia,* for example – in which the words *terrorist* and *terrorism* are not those of automatic abuse but rather the reverse, those of admiration – published in 1883 by Sergei Stepniak, an early revolutionary agitator and writer, and assassin by his own hand five years earlier of General Mezentsev, Chief of the Russian Political Police, I found a letter written dated 28th December, 1934. It was from the wife of the Soviet Ambassador to Britain, Ivan Maisky, to the then editor of the *Observer* newspaper, J.L. Garvin. The latter, described as 'prolix' by A.J.P. Taylor in his *English History 1914-1945*, and given to 'vagaries,' had sent Maisky eight volumes of Charles Greville's memoirs, from which, according to Mrs Maisky, 'my husband has spent the whole Christmas making notes.' She, on the other hand, had read the book by Stepniak, which he had also sent, which she was returning 'herewith.'

At a time when the Ukrainian famine was already raging and the British Ambassador to the Soviet Union, Sir Reader Bullard, was recording rumours of resultant cannibalism, Mrs Maisky wrote this rather florid paragraph to Garvin:

> I wish you every happiness in the New Year and most of all, vitality and energy in such quantities as will suffice to bring your life up to a thousand years.

I need hardly add that the prolongation of the human lifespan was hardly Stalin's most pressing preoccupation at the time. Stepniak called Czardom 'the Empire of the Night,' not conceiving that there could ever come into existence, let alone very soon, a regime that would go on executing more people every day for many years than the Empire of the Night executed in a hundred years. The moral is, perhaps, that we should not let the bad be the friend of the worst.

More interesting to me from my point of view as a doctor was what I found in a copy of *American Nervousness*, by George M. Beard, published in 1880. Beard was the originator of the term *neurasthenia*, a condition of chronic exhaustion found mainly among 'the in-door classes of civilized countries,' for the treatment of which he recommended, among other things, arsenic, sometimes for months, and cannabis, 'another remedy that perhaps will come [along with arsenic], one of the major divinities of neurology.' The book was inscribed by Dr Beard to Dr Ringner Atkins, a doctor of whom I have been able to discover nothing.

There was also in the book a letter addressed to Dr David Stafford-Clark, dated 7th October, 1962 from Dr Stephen MacKeith. Dr Stafford-Clark, along with Dr Anthony Storr, was the radio and television psychiatrist *par excellence*, as well as the author of many books. I can still hear in my mind's ear the cultivated upper-class English that he used. It seemed somehow to make the supposed revelations of psychoanalysis so much less shocking.

Dr MacKeith's letter, like that of Mrs Maisky, was one of thanks, ending:

> As a tiny token of my gratitude, perhaps you would accept this little book I picked up in Dublin and which I think is a first edition, inscribed by the author.

The *tininess* of the token, the *littleness* of the book, the uncertainty of its acceptability: to some these might appear the height of insincerity, or perfidious Albion writ small, but to me the totality has charm and refinement, the charm of hesitancy and indirection that has been lost in our time.

But what was Dr MacKeith grateful to Dr Stafford-Clark *for*, that necessitated what, in bibliomanic terms, was not a trifling gift?

'Dear Stafford-Clark,' the letter begins, and even this opening produced in me a *frisson* of nostalgia, for the time when men of a certain station addressed one another by their surnames (can one, for imagine, Holmes addressing Watson as John, or Watson addressing Holmes as Sherlock, let along some awful diminutive of the latter?). The letter continues:

> I send you my warmest thanks for your helpfulness on the evening of September *x*th when you came so promptly to our assistance with Mrs C.... As you may know, your prognosis was amply justified, for the following morning her mental condition was greatly improved and, indeed, was described as being better than it had been for some little time! On *n*th October, without mishap, she travelled by air back to I... and she is now back in her own home, under the wings of her husband and her remarkable old maid, Despina. I was very much impressed by your wise assessment of the clinical and social situation in this case, and by the patience and skill which you showed in dealing with the patient's husband afterwards. Incidentally, as you talked to him, you were sitting on the couch alleged once to have belonged to the famous Mrs Fitzherbert.

What doctor now would write such a letter! Doctors nowadays cannot write to each other what they really think of their patients, because they have to send copies of their letters to the patients themselves.

Then there is the letter of R.B. Cunninghame-Graham, an

author generally forgotten these days, but remembered by me for his South American writings, found in his last book, *Writ in Sand*, published in 1932. This scion of aristocratic Scottish families, who claimed to be the rightful heir to the Scottish and English thrones, ran away aged 17 to South America in search of adventure.

He knew Paraguay well, then in the aftermath of what was possibly the most disastrous war in the history of the world, at least for the male population of the losing side, namely Paraguay. Ninety-five per cent of that population was killed in the War of the Triple Alliance against Argentina, Brazil and Uruguay, and only 28,000 males were left alive in Paraguay at the end of the war.

The man most responsible for this carnage, whose inept diplomacy, Napoleonic ambition and egotistical prickliness that he mistook for honour brought it about, Marshal Francisco Solano López (son of the previous dictator of Paraguay, Carlos Antonio López, who was said by the American ambassador to Paraguay, Charles Ames Washburn, so to love his country that he owned half of it), was still a national hero when I first visited Paraguay, a large equestrian statue of him dominating the centre of Asunción, his supposedly heroic dying words inscribed on its plinth: I die with my country. The reverse was just as true, of course, my country dies with me. This is the nearest to empirical confirmation that I know of Freud's conjectured and still conjectural death wish.

It was by reading Cunninghame Graham's biography of López, the only one written in English for a century and a quarter, that I first encountered him as a writer.

King Robert IV of Scotland and the First of England, as

he sometimes liked to call himself, but also Don Roberto, was a very interesting figure, the friend alike of Bernard Shaw (who used him as the model for Serge Saranoff in *Arms and the Man*, one of the only three plays in which I have appeared on a stage, my acting abilities being approximately equal to those of an old oak beam) and Joseph Conrad, who married a woman known as Gabrielle de la Balmondière but whose real name was Caroline Horsfall, and was the first avowedly socialist Member of Parliament, an espouser of all radical causes. He spoke at meetings alongside Prince Kropotkin, Sergei Stepniak and Friedrich Engels. He was also a dandy and died a fairly rich man, leaving an estate of £100,000, the equivalent today of perhaps £6,000,000.

The dedicatory letter in the book, dated January 17, 1935 (just over a year before he died, and when he was nearly 83 years old) goes as follows:

> To A. Ll. Mattison, from R.B. Cunninghame Graham with kind regards, and in memory of the days when we used to stand on soap-boxes and address the 'Proletariat', generally composed of three or four children, eight or ten patriots from the nearest public house, two or three old women, a policeman and a lamppost.

It was written aboard the SS Windsor Castle, 'almost opposite Casa Blanca.' Morocco was Cunningham Grahame's second area of interest, after South America, and his best book, perhaps, is about it, *Mogreb-al-Acksa*.

The dedicatory letter above captures well, it seems to me, the spirit of the aristocratic radical: part generosity of spirit, part naughty boy playing his parents up by saying shocking things. The fact is that such radicals love the world and their place in it too well to want really to change it, but at the same time do not want to settle complacently into the station into which God has been good enough to call them. To do so would be unflattering to their ego, which demands that they make an impression in or on the world.

Many of them probably believe that the things that they love in the world are so solid and indestructible that their gad-fly activities cannot possibly exert any real destructive effect upon them: but by the time that they have discovered otherwise, and have wrought a world much less to their taste, it is far too late.

The most commercially valuable letter in any of my books, however, must have been pasted in by a previous owner, whoever he was. It is in a first edition of de Quincey's *Confessions of an English Opium Eater*. The letter is addressed to James Hogg Esq., Gent., whom I hoped was James Hogg, the Ettrick shepherd and author of *The Private Confessions of a Justified Sinner*, and not James Hogg, his son, the later publisher of De Quincey (who knew both father and son). How flattering to Hogg Sr it would have been, how soothing to his pride in his own achievement as a literary figure of some consequence, to have been addressed not only as *Esq.* but also as *Gent.*, by such a one as Thomas de Quincey, for he (Hogg) had been born the son of an impoverished farm worker and had received very little in the way of formal education. But de Quincey's motives in addressing him thus would not have been entirely disinterested, or arising from any sense of social equality. Here is the letter, which gives the time (12 pm) and the day and date (Thursday, August 6), but not the year:

My dear Sir,

Six weeks ago, on the 24th of June, under an alarm about my Books and Papers in Miss Millin's custody at Holyrood Gardens, – I gave her a Bill at 40 days after Date for the sum of Five Pounds. I know not how, but so it really is, that in the hurry and confusion incident to the carting away of these books, – I had forgotten the approach of this bill – an hour since it was presented to me for payment by Mr Robt Scott, of 175 High Street. Fancying that it had a fortnight still to run, – I supposed myself able to meet it by the exercise of my pen. I am ashamed of having made so childish a miscalculation. But, as the case is so, shall I appear trespassing too much on your kindness in asking you to help me out of my difficulty? I am sir
Yours very truly,
Thomas de Quincey

PS Supposing that you are kind enough to assist me in this matter, – I presume that to-morrow morning would be in time to evade [?] &c.

De Quincey's writing grows less distinct as he approaches the more difficult and embarrassing parts of his letter, until who or what he wishes to evade is altogether illegible.

I suppose some might think less well of the chronically impecunious de Quincey for having done what the vulgar would call *bumming a fiver* from Hogg, but his excuse is so transparent that it reminds one of a child – oneself, in fact, as a child – explaining why he has not handed in his homework. The ink spilt on it, and then a gust of wind made it fly out the window into the garden where the dog ate it. The more elaborate the excuse, the more the child hopes and expects some part of it to be accepted as the truth. There is something touchingly child-like about de Quincey's request; and for someone who writes, there is reassurance that literary talent and posthumous fame are not incompatible with personal weakness.

3

Enemy of the People

'People say that life is the thing,' wrote the critic, Logan Pearsall Smith, 'but I prefer reading.' On the whole, I agree. But as it happens I have a book, or rather a booklet, that was personally inscribed by the author to this all but forgotten litterateur, who is now known mainly for having been the first brother-in-law of Bertrand Russell, who wrote of him in his *Autobiography* that he was the most malicious scandal-monger whom he had ever known.

The booklet inscribed to Pearsall Smith, dated 1926, is titled *Reading: A Vice or a Virtue?* It is by the then-librarian of Northwestern University in Evanston, Illinois, Theodore Wesley Koch, whom one might have supposed to have had a vested interest in proclaiming the virtues of reading.

But librarians do not always have a straightforward or affectionate relationship either with readers or with books, especially nowadays. Indeed, some librarians seem to harbour for the books under their guardianship that special malice or hatred that people who feel trapped in their careers, and who are terminally bored by what once interested them, develop towards their tools or equipment. They cannot wait for an opportunity to wreak their vengeance on them.

This is a comparatively recent development. Librarians do not appear as one of the enemies of books in the short volume published in 1880 by the printer and literary essayist,

William Blades, titled *The Enemies of Books*. Blades lists those enemies, from the lowliest to the highest, in a kind of hierarchy or great chain of being. Starting with fire and water, he proceeds into the organic world with vegetable and then animal destroyers, working his way up through the insects to the mammals and finally to that paragon of vandals, Man himself. There is a hierarchy among men, of course, from the lowly servant who is portrayed unselfconsciously lighting a fire with pages torn from a Caxton Bible, to the worst and most destructive of all book-vandals (in Blades' opinion): the book-collector, who will do anything to a book to make it conform what he wants it, or thinks it ought, to be. Librarians in Blades' day were evidently still protectors of human civilisation.

Things have changed since then. All over Britain, and no doubt elsewhere, librarians are divesting their institutions of books. Books are bulky; books are heavy; books decay; books gather dust and emit a smell; books often remain unread on the shelves for decades at a time; above all, books are the past, like horse-drawn carriages or telegram boys delivering urgent messages by motor-cycle. There is no need of books now that they can be reduced digitally to a space infinitesimally small. If Hamlet were alive today, he would cry 'I could be bound to a Mac and count myself a king of infinite information.' At the current pace of developments, it will soon be possible for everyone to hold in the palm of his hand the whole of the Library of Congress, the British Library and the Bibliothèque Nationale. What need, then, of repositories of books?

Perhaps this is all true, but it does not account for the conduct of the librarians. One may still feel affection for artefacts that are out of date: indeed, one usually does. No, many librarians hate their books, because they feel that have entrapped them in what is now deemed a lowly and humdrum job, even if they chose the job themselves.

Booksellers have told me what librarians do to the collections in their care, once they have the green light to dispose of them. It is true that booksellers are like fishermen, they distrust each others' stories, regarding those that they tell themselves as uniquely worthy of credit; I have often been warned by booksellers not to believe what booksellers say.

One told me that he had, not long ago, happened to pass on foot a college in a small market town. The college was not celebrated for its contributions either to useful knowledge or to scholarship (by no means the same thing), but its library had somehow come by rare volumes of great value. These the bookseller now found in a skip by the kerb outside the college for, having not been consulted for many years, or even decades, they were now deemed surplus to requirements.

Recognising them at once for what they were, the bookseller went into the college and approached the chief librarian. He offered to buy the books, and she, with the commercial acumen that is one of the chief characteristics of British officialdom, at once suspected him of trying to swindle the college (by this, of course, she meant having to make a profit for a living). He persisted, however, and eventually persuaded her, against her better judgment, that part of something was better than the whole of nothing. He gave her a cheque. He later heard, through a junior member of staff of the college's library that, after his departure with the antiquarian books, she had called a meeting of her staff and told them that the next time they disposed of books they should cover them up in the skip so that no one would come and bother her.

Another bookseller told me a story about the central

library of a small provincial city: this one with quite a distinguished literary history and tradition. The central library was
being moved from its splendid old marbled quarters to relatively cramped new ones, the old quarters being now required
for the offices of bureaucrats. The size of the new quarters
meant that the numbers of books had to be reduced, and so
the chief librarian decided to disembarrass his institution of
all those old leather-bound volumes, scarcely if ever consulted by the general public of the city. One of the librarians,
slightly uneasy about the mass discarding and waste disposal
of hundred or thousands of old books, brought a few volumes to the bookseller, among them a first edition of Malthus
worth thousands. The bookseller showed it me.

Naively, I asked why the librarian chose to throw away the
books rather than sell them. I could see some kind of logic
(that of a savage, but nevertheless a logic) in removing these
unconsulted books from the shelves; but why not raise money
by selling them?

The answer, said the bookseller, was simple. There was a
rule in the council that, if anything belonging to it worth more
than £100 were sold, the sale had to be approved by the council. Clearly this would be impossible where hundreds, perhaps
thousands, of individual items were concerned. The council
would soon be doing nothing else but approving the sale of
its books. Far better, from the point of view of efficiency and
time management, to dispose of them as if they were super-
market wrapping or the disused cans of soft drinks.

Because of the importance, one might almost say the
sacred quality, of books in the development and transmission
of our civilisation, the wilful destruction of books has always
appeared a barbaric act. If we saw a man deliberately tearing

a book to shreds, even one without any great value, a trashy novel say, we would think him a brute. But the destruction of books *en masse* by the public authorities has never augured well for civilisation, let alone for freedom.

Books are as much the source, or instrument, of folly and evil as of wisdom and goodness; James I, an immensely well-read man, was regarded the wisest fool in Christendom, and Lenin derived from books a lot of fuel (in the form of rationalisation) for the furnace of the hatred that was his deepest motive. But, 'Wherever they burn books,' wrote Heine, 'they will also, in the end, burn human beings.' The preservation of books is an implicit recognition of the human condition: that knowledge and wisdom inevitably emerge, if they emerge at all, from ignorance and folly, that of our ancestors who were no less intelligent than we, and that it is best that we should never forget our humble origins.

No doubt the reduction of the municipal library's collection of old books to rubbish in the most literal sense was not to be compared in point of savagery with the most famous book-burning episode of modern history, that in Nazi Germany in 1933. But can a civilisation stand when those who are supposed to be among its most active guardians or protectors insidiously involve themselves, apparently without conscience, in the destruction of that civilisation's resources of memory?

I have given two instances of barbaric librarianship. Unfortunately there are other instances known to me. To say that I could multiply them indefinitely would be an exaggeration, because my collection has been made casually, without any special effort. Yet another bookseller told me, for example, of a time when he was called to a municipality's central library to make an offer to buy its ancient books. He found the books, from the seventeenth to the nineteenth centuries, strewn on the floor and the staff actually walking over them, as if they were treading grapes for wine. (Many a reluctant pupil or student has carried a book by his side for hours on end without ever opening it, in the hope that its contents will somehow enter his brain by a process of osmosis. I have done it myself.) He wrote a cheque to save these books from their pedestrian fate, and was surprised to discover a few months later that it had gone uncashed.

4

The Glow of Angels

Even the greatest minds have sometimes to turn on to trivial objects. In my copy of Samuel Rogers' *Human Life: A Poem*, of 1819, I found a letter on fading lavender paper written in a spidery hand to the following effect:

My dear Charles,

Pray breakfast with me, if it is in your power, on Wednesday next at <u>10</u> precisely.
S. Rogers
St James' Place
Monday

If I hear nothing, I shall venture to hope. The garden gate will be open.

Samuel Rogers is, of course, not a name on everyone's lips, and is probably all but unknown even to people well-versed in the literature of that era. But in his day he was of great literary importance and reputation. According to the *Dictionary of National Biography*, this banker, who read the poems of Thomas Gray on his way to the bank – where he became very rich – 'won a high place among the poets of his age, through the careful polishing of a minor talent' (a phrase to strike fear into the heart of any writer).

Works by men of minor talent can endure, of course, but mainly if they are the lesser manifestations of an *avant garde* movement. It was Rogers' misfortune, from the point of view of his lasting reputation, that he was the last of the Augustan poets precisely at a time when Romanticism was at the flood. In the end, he became what the *Dictionary* calls 'a literary potentate' by running a salon and lending writers money, more celebrated for whom he knew and what he had lent than for what he had written.

Human Life is a seven-ages-of-man poem in heroic couplets:

> After all the vicissitudes of life, death comes at
> the last.
> Then was the drama ended. Not till then,
> So full of chance and change the lives of men,
> Could we pronounce him happy. Then secure
> From pain, from grief, and all that we endure,
> He slept in peace – ...

This stoic consolation, that death is not so much oblivion as a prolonged, hard-won and happy philosophic peace, is somehow ill-assorted with the urgency of Charles' instruction to come at 10 o'clock precisely, the figure 10 in the letter being scored several times in ink.

Of course, Rogers was a banker as well as a litterateur, and had business to conduct; but even banks are of small importance measured against eternities of time and space. You can look up at the stars and descant on the pettiness and insignificance of human existence as much as you like, but you will still be irritated if the train is late.

And this brings to mind Imlac's wise injunction to Rasselas, in Johnson's fable: 'Be not too hasty to trust, or to admire, the teachers of morality; they discourse like angels, but they live like men.'

I was taught another lesson by an uninteresting letter by an author whom I dare not call famous, but who is well-known to those who know him well, Sir Sidney Lee.

Lee, born with the name Solomon in 1858 to a Jewish family in England, was the most famous Shakespeare scholar of his day and second editor of the *Dictionary of National Biography*. Bookish from an early age and a lifelong bachelor, he was already known for his learning, not to say his pedantry, as an undergraduate at Balliol, where the following lines were written of him:

> My gown, the wonder of beholders,
> Hangs like a footnote from my shoulders.

I bought a copy of Lee's *Life of William Shakespeare* in one of those very few country towns in England whose beauty has not been comprehensively destroyed by a combination of professional town planning and modernist architecture, after attending a murder trial there as an expert witness. The number of ways of classifying books being infinite, I could have a little section in my library called 'Books bought after examining or attending the trial of murderers, while waiting for the train home.'

Lee's life is still a standard work, after more than a hundred years; the edition in the second-hand shop was the fourth, marked in pencil by the bookseller as 'the fourth, and best.' (To say of a book that its particular edition is the best is the bookseller's apology for it not being rare or much sought after by those who like only rarities.)

The bookshop in the county town was minded by a type increasingly rare in Britain: the shy, polite, educated, modest, bookish young man in slightly down-at-heel tweeds or corduroy, the type who apologises to you when you tread on his toes. It being a sunny day, his boss, the owner of the shop, to whom, from respect, he referred as Mr Smith rather than by his Christian name (let alone a diminutive of it), was sitting sunning himself on a chair outside, smoking a pipe filled with sweetish tobacco. He was a genial, elderly man whom one would have taken for a sailor rather than for a bookseller.

The book was marked at £20, and I felt it only right to point out that there was a letter by Sir Sidney Lee in it – of no intrinsic or historical interest, except that it was his.

'Had you noticed this?' I asked, showing the young man the letter. 'It might affect the price.'

'I don't think we did notice it,' said the young man. 'I'd better ask the owner, Mr Smith.'

He went out to ask Mr Smith, and indeed Mr Smith had not noticed it.

'Does it affect the price?' asked the young man.

'Yes,' said Mr Smith. 'Eighteen pounds.'

It was absurd, no doubt, to be so deeply cheered by this generous recognition of honesty; but suddenly I felt that humanity was better that I had given it credit for being. No doubt it was the influence of the sunny day as well being in so pleasant a town, but I walked to the station with a spring in my step.

Of course, it helped that I had been well-paid as an expert witness. This helped me to disremember, as a modern politician might have put it, the sordidness of the murder case in the trial of which I had just appeared. So when I look at the letter by Sir Sidney Lee, a warm glow of benevolent feeling still comes over me, a bit like the warmth in my gullet when I drink brandy.

5

Mrs Buggins

I have, for example, two books that I keep together, though of widely divergent subject matter, that are interleaved – that is to say, with extra pages bound in with hand-written commentary on the text upon them. The first is my copy of *An Inquiry into the Physiological and Medicinal Properties of the Aconitum Napellus to which Are Added Observations on Several other Species of Aconitum* by Alexander Fleming, published in 1845.

Perhaps this sounds a somewhat dry volume, but it is very far from being so. In the first place, it belonged to Alexander Fleming (1823-75) himself, and also to a man called Gamgee. Since Fleming moved from Edinburgh to Cork, where he was Professor of Materia Medica, and then to Birmingham, where he was professor of the same subject, it is likely that the Gamgee to which it belonged was Joseph Sampson Gamgee, the eminent surgeon of Birmingham who, among other things, invented the absorbent sanitary towel for women.

Included in the volume when I bought it was a small pamphlet, printed in 1848 in Edinburgh, entitled *Testimonials in Favour of Alexander Fleming, M.D., Candidate for the Chair of Materia Medica in One of the Queen's Colleges, Ireland*, obviously at the candidate's own expense, and directed at the Chief Secretary for Ireland, in whose gift the chair lay. Fleming put forward his candidacy, which was successful, only four years after graduating, and during the middle of the Irish potato famine.

The pamphlet not only has testimonials from several famous doctors of his day, including James Young Simpson, the discoverer of chloroform anaesthesia, but extracts of reviews of his book on aconite, including one in the *Dublin Journal of Medical Science* for September 1845, while thousands of people were dying of hunger not far from where it was written:

> We look upon his inquiry as a most valuable contribution to that important, though strangely neglected, branch of practical medicine – therapeutics.

I had always supposed that boastfulness about one's accomplishments, as the means of getting on and climbing ever higher in the medical profession, was of recent origin, but it appears not. I happened to see the end of a brief interlude when people left it to others to blow their trumpet; but it is once again a bureaucratic requirement (even from the point of view of mere survival, let alone advancement) that one rehearse one's accomplishments in public.

Fleming was the greatest expert of his time (perhaps of any time) on aconite, or wolfsbane. He was the inventor of Fleming's tincture, a solution of the drug that he recommended as an analgesic and as a symptomatic treatment for a large variety of diseases, from headache to tetanus. The text of his book is strewn with commentary, as if in preparation of a second edition (which was never published): for

example, with a question mark with the words in his handwriting 'Is this true?' in the opposite margin, or 'frequently'
scored out and 'occasionally' written above it.
Unfortunately, his handwriting in his longer commentary is
indecipherable, at least by me: I can make out 'Mrs Buggins,
Worcester, May, 1871,' but not – alas – what it was that Mrs
Buggins of Worcester said or did. According to the census
of April, 1871, there were two Mrs Bugginses living in
Worcester.

The most intriguing section of the book relates to poisoning by aconite, accidental and criminal. It is a strange
fact that criminal poisoning by aconite is very rare, though
the plant from the leaves and root of which the poison is
extracted is widespread and extraction is easy. In this section, Dr Fleming pasted in contemporary press reports of
poisoning with aconite, the most interesting of which, perhaps, was that of Dr George Edward Male, known as the
father of English forensic medicine, for he wrote the first
original textbook in English on the subject.

In 1845, when he was 66 years old, Dr Male, having read
Dr Fleming's book, and suffering from rheumatic pains in
the joints for which Dr Fleming advocated the use of tincture of aconite, took the recommended dose for several
days. Under the heading 'Death of Dr Male, of
Birmingham,' in the *Medical Times* of August 9, 1845 (the
publication and date inscribed by Dr Fleming), we read:

> It appears that Dr Male had for some time
> prior to his decease been the subject of severe
> rheumatic pains, for which he had tried, but
> unavailingly, a variety of remedies; at last it

occurred to him, on reading a work recently published by Dr Fleming on Aconite, to make trial of that drug.

His doctor was called when he began to be unwell; 'he expressed [to his doctor] his conviction that he should die, that the medicine was too powerful for him; but he also expressed his most earnest desire that he should recover, as his life was of the utmost importance to his children at this time.'

The doctor returned on the evening of the following day, and 'found him in a dying state. He was in a torpid condition, from which, however, he could be easily roused, and then his intellect was clear. He had no paralysis; he was perfectly composed and died about ten o'clock [the following morning].'

There followed an encomium to the deceased, the most memorable part of which is as follows:

> Perhaps the best proof of the estimation in which he was held by the profession of Birmingham, will be found in a remark made to the writer of this article by a fellow-physician, who is too just to pay an unmerited compliment, and too generous to withhold a deserved one – the observation came with peculiar emphasis, for it was offered over a grave – 'Dr Male, Sir, was a man to whom I invariably took my hat off.'

But I, in turn, take my hat off to Dr Fleming, for having had the honesty to insert an article into his own copy of his book about a death for which he must have felt it in part responsible.

I do not know whether his actual practice was affected by the case of Dr Male, but the first person to whom one must admit something discreditable is oneself, or else all is lost. On the first page interleaved, he write what appears to be a preliminary note for a preface to the second edition (which never saw the light of day):

> In <u>preface</u> – say – my endeavour was always to find out its great activity and [illegible] for caution, I have shown this, the reason why I introduced cases where action was carried too far.

More than a century and a half later, however, Dr Fleming's book (which incidentally it would have taken £1 to buy in 1956, according to a bookseller's catalogue of that year) played a small part in bringing a murderer to justice.

Bringing a murderer to justice doesn't quite compensate for the death of a patient, of course; but it nevertheless showed that Dr Fleming's book, on a subject on which no more recent book has been published, at least in English, still has scientific value – for knowledge can be lost, or rather forgotten, as well as gained.

It so happened that a friend of mine, a professor of clinical pharmacology with an interest in murder by poison, visited me in France (where most of my library now is) while he had been retained by the prosecution in a case of suspected aconite poisoning, the first in Britain since 1882, when Dr George Henry Lamson was hanged for having poisoned his crippled brother-in-law with aconitine (the poison principle of aconite), in order to lay his hands on his legacy.

The man who died in this case had all the symptoms of

aconite poisoning, but no aconite was found in his body. My friend then had the brilliant idea that he had been killed not with the poison derived from the common-or-garden English *Aconitum napellus*, but with poison derived from the Indian *Aconitum ferox*, a chemical very similar to but distinct from, though with all the same clinical effects as, aconitine, a chemical known as pseudo-aconitine. (The accused was from a family of Indian descent.) And pseudoaconitine was duly found in the deceased's body. A case that had all but collapsed in frustration was saved.

My friend, who was soon to go into the witness-box, wanted to fore-arm himself with all the information possible on this kind of poisoning, and Fleming still had by far the best and most detailed clinical accounts of it. And in due course the woman was convicted, her account of how pseudoaconitine had found itself into her ex-lover's curry not being believed.

The second of my interleaved books is on quite another subject: Henry Edwards Davis' sonorously-titled *An Examination of the Fifteenth and Sixteenth Chapters of Mr. Gibbon's History of the Decline and Fall of the Roman Empire in which His View of the Progress of the Christian Religion Is Shewn to be Founded on the Misrepresentation of the Authors He Cites: And Numerous Instances of His Inaccuracy and Plagiarism Are Produced.*

Davis was 22 years old when he produced this challenge to Gibbon, and at least he cannot be accused of having used a misleading title or of having failed to put his cards straight on

the table. In his chapters XV and XVI Gibbon, of course, had
been ironically disparaging about the spread of Christianity in
the ancient world, attributing it more to normal, that is to say
discreditable, human motives than to what he calls 'the truth
of the doctrine itself.' In reply, Henry Edwards Davis (who
was only one of several detractor's of Gibbon's great book)
did not mince his words:

> On examining his [Gibbon's] references, when
> they are to be traced, we shall find him support-
> ing his cause by manifest falsification, and per-
> petually assuming to himself the strange privi-
> lege of inserting into his text what the writers
> referred to give him no right to advance on their
> authority... I shall be able to lay before my read-
> ers, proofs as flagrant as they are numerous, that
> if he had consulted the authors only with a view
> to misrepresent them, he could scarcely have
> deviated more from plain truth, than he now
> does.

In short, Gibbon was an unprincipled liar.

Gibbon, who called Davis' title page 'a declaration of war,'
replied in his *A Vindication of Some Passages in the Fifteenth and
Sixteenth Chapters of the History of the Decline and Fall of the
Roman Empire*. He, too, did not mince his words:

> Every animal employs the note, or cry, or howl,
> which is peculiar to its species; every man
> expresses himself in the dialect the most con-
> genial to his temper and inclination, the most

familiar to the company in which he has lived,
and to the authors with whom he is conver-
sant...

The general opinion is that Gibbon gave Davis a good intellectual and literary caning in his *Vindication*, to which Davis,
unwilling to admit defeat, nevertheless responded with his
own *A Reply to Mr Gibbon's Vindication*: but the name of
Gibbon lives on, while that of Davis is completely unknown
except to specialists in the literary history of the period.

My learned annotator (whose identity I will never know,
but whose beautiful, slender, elegant, cultivated hand in
English, Latin and Greek I shall always admire) is generally on
the side of Davis, whose defeat may not have seemed as evident at the time as it has seemed to posterity. The annotator
is mostly on the side of Davis, but not uncritically so, for
sometimes he writes such comments as 'Of this borrow'd
Misrepresentation Mr G. prudently takes no notice in his
Vindication,' or 'Mr D. [Davis] has here very unfortunately
mistaken Eusebius,' or 'This charge is not accurate.'

He even corrects young Davis' language once or twice, in
the manner of a pouncing pedant, at once exasperated and
delighted by the error that he has found: in the margin against
'He tells us indeed that the Pharisees really believed in a res-
urrection, and such a one as the gospel taught...,' for example, is inscribed, 'such an one,' both 'a one' and 'an' in 'an one'
being underlined, the only time in all his copious annotations
that the annotator resorts to the technique of underlining.
One can just imagine him shaking his head in sorrow that
young people nowadays do not know how to write even their
own language properly. I hasten to add that the mere fact that

the annotator was unjustified in his complaint in 1779 does not mean that the same complaint is not justified now. One does not say of an earthquake that it has not happened simply because seismologists years ago repeatedly and mistakenly warned of its imminence.

But the annotator expresses his agreement with David far more often than his disagreement. Often he simply writes 'No defence' in the margin, where he thinks that Gibbon's *Vindication* did not answer the charge against him; but sometimes he writes at slightly lengthier asperity:

> See his shuffling evasion

Or:

> Mr Gibbon attempts to defend his translation, but notwithstanding all he says, is such a one, as no unprejudiced man could have adopted...

Or again:

> Mr G's Attempt to Vindicate himself from Misrepresentation here proceeds on either Misapprehensions or Misrepresentations, and ends in a compliment to his own Candor, for giving a wrong sense to a Greek word.

Gibbon here stands accused of translating the Greek word for *false accusation* as *accusation*, and it is not easy for a non-scholar to adjudicate between the parties; even a scholar might require some time to do so, and it is possible that there is no indubitable solution to the controversy, only a balance of probability. David Wormersley, the greatest contemporary Gibbon scholar and editor of what is generally acknowledged to be the best edition of *The Decline and Fall*, says of the controversy in his biography of Gibbon in the *Dictionary of National Biography*:

> The *Vindication* was Gibbon's only public engagement with his detractors and, in the opinion of all but the detractors themselves, his victory was complete.

But the annotator does not seem to be aware of this. A learned man, he appears also to have been a scrupulous and honest one. No doubt he had his prejudices, but who does not?

Unaware of the judgment of posterity – that Gibbon's victory was complete – he tried to judge for himself, and came to the wrong conclusion (assuming posterity to have been right). This is an implicit call to modesty, one that is seldom heeded, least of all by me.

It is possible to know a great deal, and yet be mistaken about the very subject of one's knowledge. Thus we always see through a glass darkly, yet pronounce on everything as if our eyes were at one and the same time the most powerful microscopes and telescopes possible.

6

How to Be Colour Blind

Criminal poisoning features quite highly in a particular category of books in my library: those of suppressed modern first editions. This category might well be larger in Britain than some other countries, thanks to the nature of our libel laws.

I have, for example, a copy of the first edition of Robert Graves' *Goodbye to All That*, the edition which Siegfried Sassoon insisted upon pain of a libel suit that the publishers should suppress. I also have the first edition of Graham Greene's *Journey without Maps*, which was pulped by the publishers under threat by Dr P D Oakley of a libel action (though most of the copies had by then been sold). Dr Oakley, a colonial medical officer in Sierra Leone, objected to the character in the book of Pa Oakley, who was portrayed as a drunken and bigoted vulgarian. Greene denied that Pa Oakley was P.D. Oakley, but to no avail: there were presumably few other Oakleys in Sierra Leone at the time.

Poor Dr Oakley died in obscurity in 1958, aged 75, while his detractor (if that is what he was) went from national to world fame. All I have found out about Dr Oakley is that he passed his anatomy and physiology exams in 1906, received his diploma in tropical medicine in 1920, was Director of Medical Services in Sierra Leone and was decorated in 1936 (the year of Greene's book) for his work there, was Transport Medical Officer and Medical-Officer in-Charge of

Evacuation Trains 1939-1946, died in 1958 in Sussex, was survived 14 years by his widow, and had an only son, who died in 2003 aged 86, who was a career naval officer.

Skeletal as this knowledge of the man is, it makes it unlikely that he could have served as the model for Pa Oakley. He was probably intelligent and diligent, and quite possibly more actively and consistently concerned for the welfare of mankind than Greene. But he was without that spark of genius that carries a man's name from one age to the next.

But three of my suppressed books concern poisonings and poisoners, two of them about the same man, Dr John Bodkin Adams. Dr Adams was a Northern Irish evangelical Christian doctor of the Plymouth Brethren sect, a lifelong bachelor, who was a general practitioner in Eastbourne, the somewhat staid town on the South coast of England to which respectable and moneyed folk went, and still go, to retire and die.

Dr Adams made himself thoroughly at home among the private hotels, boarding houses and residences in which widows lived out their last years. When they died, it was found that many of them (132 in total) had remembered Dr Adams in their wills; and rumours began to circulate that Dr Adams had been helping them on their way. As he later termed it in a splendidly unctuous phrase, he had been 'easing the passing.'

The rumours were persistent; even before the war Dr Adams used regularly to receive anonymous postcards accusing him of murder. Eventually, bodies of Dr Adams' former patients were exhumed and found to contain large quantities of heroin and other opiate drugs, and Dr Adams was charged with murder by poison.

Before the trial in 1957, a masterpiece of comic poetry,

whose author has never been discovered but which deserves to be better known, circulated in Eastbourne. The police, fearing it might prejudice the trial, tried vainly to suppress it:

In Eastbourne it is healthy
And the residents are wealthy
It's a miracle that anybody dies;
Yet this pearl of English lidos
Is a slaughter house of widows –
If their bank rolls are above the normal size.
If they're lucky in addition
In their choice of a physician
And remember him when making out their wills
And bequeath their Rolls Royces
Then they soon hear angel voices
And are quickly freed from all their earthly ills…
    As we witness the deceased borne
    From the stately homes of Eastbourne
We are calm, for it may safely be assumed
That each lady that we bury
In the local cemetery
    Will re-surface – when the body is exhumed.
    It's the mortuary chapel
    If they touch an Adam's apple
    After parting with a Bentley as a fee.
    So to liquidate your odd kin
    By the needle of the bodkin
    Send them down to sunny Eastbourne by the sea.

Here, perhaps, I permit myself a little nostalgia. The relation of the British, and especially the English, to their murders is, or rather was, one of their salient national characteristics. It is, or was, simultaneously prurient and ironical. No nation, I think, was ever so devoted to reading the transcripts of the trials of murderers as the British; and if I had to point to a date at which British culture ceased to have any worthwhile distinguishing features, I should put it at 1959, when the last in the series *Notable British Trials*, the eighty-third, of the Edinburgh firm of William Hodge and Company, was published.

These red cloth-covered books make the most wonderful reading; they appeal equally to the normal human desire for the sensational and the dramatic as to that for genuine understanding of human nature. Greed, cruelty, sexual passion, insensate hatred, evil incarnate since birth, pathos and bathos: all are recorded and dissected in them. They are in themselves a complete course of human psychology.

The magnificent speeches both for the defence and the prosecution, help to explain why the prominent advocates of the time were household names, their fame now having passed to less worthy or considerable recipients; the miscarriages of justice – for several such there were – exercise a cathartic effect on the reader as strong as that of any literature known to me.

Moreover, each of the transcripts of the trials is furnished with a long introduction by a man or woman (one of them, F. Tennyson Jesse, a great-niece of Alfred, Lord Tennyson) who wrote the most excellent prose. Indeed, if anyone were to ask me what he should read in order to learn how to write good prose, I might very well recommend the introductions to the *Notable British Trials* series.

In thousands of pages, there is scarcely a dull page. At random, I open my copy of *Trial of George Joseph Smith*, edited by Eric R. Watson, on page 50. Smith was the infamous Brides in the Bath murderer, who in 1915 was convicted of having drowned three bigamously-married brides in order to steal their money. Not particularly well-favoured by nature, he nevertheless had no difficulty in seducing women prior to killing them and then persuading doctors that they had drowned during epileptic fits. Under the heading *Studies in Psychology*, the editor of the *Trial* editor states:

> The fascination which very depraved men exer-
> cise over women has long stimulated criminolo-
> gists to discover – hitherto with little success –
> what common attribute bad men possess which
> makes them so ingratiating to the sex.

Perhaps no one would dare any longer raise such a question, pressure groups now exercising more censorship than mere governments; but it is a fact (if my experience as prison doctor is anything to go by) that notorious criminals, those whose terrible and vicious exploits reach the newspapers, seldom lack for declarations of love and offers of marriage from women who have never met them. And, indeed, many a noto-rious killer has married in prison, sometimes to a psychologist. Petty criminals – shoplifters, unsuccessful burglars – do not, by contrast, attract in the same way.

Perhaps the question should be what characteristic is com-mon to women who are attracted to bad men rather than what is the characteristic of bad men that attracts women to them. After all, not *all*, only a very small minority of, women are attracted to bad men. Indeed, in Smith's case, it seems that he either seduced or produced a very strong feeling of revulsion in those who met him. The first time he married, under the assumed name of Love, shortly after meeting his bride for the first time, his in-laws had so disliked him at first sight that they refused to attend the ceremony.

Why was the reaction of the parents to him so different from that of the bride (and, as it turned out, founded on so much more accurate an assessment of his character)? Was it that she, the bride, failed to see in him what her parents saw, like those people in America who do not see what is obvious to everybody else, that the television evangelists to whom they send money are crooks and charlatans? Do some people have a faculty of divining evil in others that other people lack, as in a kind of moral colour-blindness?

I certainly would not like to give the impression that the whole of the distinctness of British culture rested on the shoulders of William Hodge and Company. The publication of transcripts of trials was a tradition at least three hundred years old when it died, and its death was abrupt rather than gradual.

Other companies published series such as William Hodge and Company's: Geoffrey Bles, for example. My favourite among these is *The Trial of Norman Thorne* of 1929, which in its subtitle assumes the familiarity of the public with the case: *The Crowborough Chicken-Farm Murder*. This is the kind of readers' familiarity that glossy celebrity magazines assume when they write of the break-up of Jason's relationship with Charlene. one already knows who Jason and Charlene are, which is why their break-up is supposedly of interest. (I cannot help thinking that an interest in old-fashioned murder is far healthier and more intelligent than an interest in modern-day celebrities.)

The *Trial of Norman Thorne* was edited by Helena Normanton, the first woman barrister to reach the top of her profession (she also edited a volume in the other series). Her account of the Crowborough Chicken-Farm Murder starts as follows:

> On the morning of December 5th, 1924, a young woman named Elsie Cameron was having her hair waved at her hairdresser's. On her return home she attired herself in a new jumper and shortly after midday departed from her parents' house in Kensal Rise for her lover's dwelling near Crowborough. She believed that she was taking her nuptial journey, and awaited marriage as its result. Before twenty-four hours had passed the neatly coiffured head had been severed from her shoulders and buried in an old tin in one of the chicken runs on her sweetheart's farm, her dismembered torso have been interred beside it. Such was her journey, such her fate.

I defy anyone to read that paragraph and not read on.

Of course, it is not just the transcripts of murder that have declined, but the murders themselves. This was pointed out as long ago as 1946 by George Orwell, in his essay *The Decline of the English Murder*, and what he said then is even more true now. The decline of Britain as an intensely law-abiding society into one of the most criminally-inclined in the western world has rendered murder merely crude and sordid, in a word *ordinary*.

Orwell accurately described what it was about the *causes célèbres* of the previous era that rendered them so intensely interesting, and he brilliantly extracted those elements of a murder that went to make it the perfect crime (from the William Hodge and Company point of view):

> The murderer should be a little man of the professional class—a dentist or a solicitor, say—living an intensely respectable life somewhere in the suburbs, and preferably in a semi-detached house, which will allow the neighbours to hear suspicious sounds through the wall. He should be either chairman of the local Conservative Party branch, or a leading Nonconformist and strong Temperance advocate. He should go astray through cherishing a guilty passion for his secretary or the wife of a rival professional man, and should only bring himself to the point of murder after long and terrible wrestles with his conscience. Having decided on murder, he should plan it all with the utmost cunning, and only slip up over some tiny unforeseeable detail. The means chosen should, of course, be poison. In the last analysis he should commit murder because this seems to him less disgraceful, and less damaging to his career, than being detected in adultery. With this kind of background, a crime can have dramatic and even tragic qualities which make it memorable and excite pity for both victim and murderer.

What appealed to Orwell about Smith, the brides-in-the-bath murderer, was that, while one of his victims lay drowned next door, he played the hymn *Nearer, My God, to Thee*, on the harmonium.

In a society, however, in which there is no non-conformist respectability, there can be no unexpected outrage of it. Drug dealers shooting one another are not of much interest, and one cares little about the victim or the perpetrator, neither of whom is interesting. It is true that I once arrived on the intensive care unit of my hospital to find it populated by policemen with automatic weapons, guarding two drug dealers who had shot one another, not fatally but causing sufficient wounds to require intensive care. This was, indeed, a situation of some interest, at least potentially: for the moment, they were both paralysed and on ventilators. There will be no revival, I fear, of *Notable British Trials*. Our attention span is too limited, our crimes too frequent.

Ah, where are the murderers of yesterday?

7

But Is It Safe?

Let us return to Dr John Bodkin Adams, the Eastbourne poisoner. His name, of course, and also his face (round, pudgy, bespectacled, faintly smirking and sinister), could hardly have been better contrived for a murder of the Hodge and Company-Orwell type. As someone who appears from time to time in our courts as an expert witness, I learned a lot from reading reports of the trial.

The chief medical witness for the prosecution was a distinguished physician, Dr Arthur Douthwaite, who was, from the prosecution's point of view, a complete disaster.

He argued that Bodkin Adams' use of heroin could only have been with murderous intent, which was plainly well beyond anything that he could justify by the evidence that he had; and, in a brilliant cross-examination by Geoffrey Lawrence, QC, whose first criminal trial this was, admitted that he had decided on Bodkin Adams' guilt and then fitted all the facts around it. Douthwaite was exactly what an expert witness should not be, impartiality being replaced completely by advocacy. On the evidence presented in the trial, no jury could have done anything except acquit.

Dr Bodkin Adams' acquittal turned out to be another source of income to him. First he sold his story to the *Daily Express* for £10,000 – a great deal of money in those days. Then he sued publications whenever they described him as a murderer, and always won.

Two books were suppressed soon after publication by their publishers, on threat of libel action by Bodkin Adams, because they described him as a murderer. The first was the fourth in a series of volumes titled *Famous Criminal Cases*, by the journalist, Rupert Furneaux, which was published annually between 1954 and 1962, giving brief accounts of the previous year's most notorious crimes. It ceased publication thereafter, perhaps because the author grew bored with it, or, more likely, because the inexorable rise of crime made the very notion of notorious crimes anachronistic. Where crime is normal, nothing will be notorious. The fourth volume in the series, however, was withdrawn because it described Bodkin Adams as a murderer, though a few got into circulation, and is now much rarer and more expensive than the other volumes.

In 1963, the great writer of political thrillers, Eric Ambler, published a pot-boiler about the psychology of murder called *The Ability to Kill*. (It was the dedicatee of this, my book, who once pointed out to me how good the prose was of popular authors of the 1930s and 40s, and even that of pulp fiction writers of that era.) In *The Ability to Kill* Ambler described, briefly, many murderers, including the subject of one of my small collections, Dr William Palmer of Rugeley in Staffordshire, known to contemporaries as the Prince of Poisoners. Dr Palmer was hanged outside Stafford gaol in 1856 before a crowd of 20-30,000 (the population of the town at the time having been 10,000). He probably poisoned fourteen people with antimony or strychnine, including his own children, best friend and mother-in-law, all for money; his picture still adorns some of the local pubs, for lack of any other local hero. As he was led to the scaffold before the howling mob, he saw that the scaffold had been hastily constructed, and turned to the executioner and asked 'Is it safe?' Try as one might to keep in mind his wickedness, one cannot help but admire somewhat a man who goes to his death jauntily enough to make so amusing and ironical a remark to the very man charged with ending his life – assuming that the remark was ironical.

My best item, perhaps, of Palmeriana is the open letter that the Reverend Thomas Palmer addressed to the Lord Chief Justice, who tried William Palmer, in the week before Palmer's execution, of which very few copies are known to exist. It is entitled *A Letter to the Lord Chief Justice Campbell, Containing Remarks upon the Conduct of the Prosecution and the Judges; with Strictures on the Charge Delivered to the Jury, Illustrative of its Dangerous Tendencies to the Long-enjoyed Rights and Privileges of Englishmen.* Thomas Palmer is described on the title page (as if it were an academic qualification) as *Brother to the Prisoner, William Palmer*, but according to the first edition of the *Dictionary of National Biography* he subsequently denied having written it. This seems to me likely; for not even the natural partiality of brotherhood could account for the grotesque misdescription of William Palmer's character, whose life's work and claim to fame are abbreviated in the current edition of the *DNB* as *Poisoner and Physician* (a lamentably large category), as follows:

> From childhood upward, no man was gentler of heart, his charity was inexhaustible; his kindliness to all who were in distress was well known.

> To him the wanderer resorted in his afflictions;
> by him the poor and houseless were fed and
> comforted.

Short of outright political propaganda in dictatorships that
extols the beauty of the personality of the dictator, there has
scarcely ever have been a less apt or accurate character sketch
of anyone than this; for even if innocent of murder, there is
abundant evidence that Palmer, though a doctor, was an
unmitigated scoundrel. But the letter, 48 pages long, with
another 34 pages of supporting documents, is eloquently
written and does at least make out a case that Lord Chief
Justice Campbell conducted the trial at the Old Bailey in a
scandalously biased fashion: a charge that history, which is to
say the majority of those who write it, has in general accepted. Indeed, Robert Graves, who wrote an historical novel
about the case, titled *They Hanged My Saintly Billy* (a title that is
taken from what William Palmer's mother exclaimed when
she was told that he had been hanged), must have used
Thomas Palmer's *Letter* in coming to the conclusion that his
brother was indeed innocent.

Be that all as it may, Ambler had to withdraw his book and
replace the chapter on Bodkin Adams by another. It is said
that only fifty copies of the original version escaped destruction by pulping, and therefore, when I handle my copy of this
otherwise not very distinguished book, I experience the thrill
of the miser who hugs his gold to him, not so much enjoying
it for what it can do for him as for the fact that his possession
of it denies it to someone else. There are few pleasures more
reliable, though illicit, than that of denying things to others.
This is not creditable, but it is human.

Before I leave the subject of Bodkin Adams and the books he managed to suppress by threat of libel action, I will mention a puzzle about him which I have not seen referred to by others: namely, why he left so little money. He died in 1984, leaving £400,000, a respectable sum but certainly not a huge one. Now very early in his career, when property was cheap, he bought an eighteen-room mansion in Eastbourne, which in 1984, when he was still living in it, must have been worth a great deal; in 1937 he inherited the equivalent in 1984 of £400,000 from a patient, which wisely or even only competently invested would be a fortune nearly half a century later; and while some of his 132 legacies might have been comparatively small, nevertheless the total, when you consider that some of them included Rolls-Royce cars and canteens of silver, must have been considerable. All this time, he was practising as a successful doctor, and therefore earning well; and, apart from the size of his house, his lifestyle was not extravagant. He also received several large libel settlements. His estate was therefore much smaller than one might have expected. Why?

Though every picture of him that I have seen of him makes him look thoroughly untrustworthy if not outright sinister (though, of course, I come to those pictures with a biased mind), Bodkin Adams must have had charm, and maybe other qualities, for when he was removed from the medical register for a time and not allowed to practise, many of his patients continued to consult him even though he could not prescribe any but over-the-counter medicines for them that they could have bought themselves without him as an intermediary. Suspicion that he murdered his patients – suspicions, after all, that had circulated for thirty years at least in a town like Eastbourne, where nothing could have been secret for very long – did nothing to reduce the loyalty of his patients to him, indeed, in a perverse kind of way, might actually have increased it. For a few patients there might have been a pleasant frisson of danger in consulting him; others would have taken a pride in so conspicuously taking no notice of mere tittle-tattle and gossip. In continuing to consult Dr Bodkin Adams they were displaying their moral superiority, their British fair-mindedness.

Dr Bodkin Adams was also, for a time, honorary president of the British Clay Pigeon Shooting Association. He must therefore have charmed members of that association (he was a keen shot himself). And it seems to have been the case that he was kind to the poor, insofar as anyone in Eastbourne was poor, treating them with solicitude; he was also charitable. Could it be, in fact, that he gave most of his fortune away? If this is so, he *certainly* obeyed the injunction in Matthew's 6:1 to do his good works mostly out of the sight of others.

He might even have been the Robin Hood *de nos jours*, inheriting money from the Eastbourne rich to give it to the poor.

8

Good People and Stuff

The last book about poisoning that I have whose first edition, in 1971, was suppressed because of threat of libel action was that of *The Young Poisoner*, by Anthony Holden. In this case, the libel action was threatened not by the poisoner, who had no reputation to lose, but by the staff of Broadmoor Hospital, who objected to the way in which they were depicted in the book.

The poisoner, Graham Young, was a curious man, who almost certainly poisoned his stepmother to death when he was fourteen years old. He developed an obsessive interest in poisons at the age of eleven and it remained with him for the rest of his life. He poisoned, though not fatally, his best friend, his father, and his sister, and was probably a great admirer of none other than William Palmer.

When he was first caught, he was declared criminally insane and sent to Broadmoor, where it was rumoured that he killed a man by extracting cyanide from the leaves of laurel bushes in the hospital grounds. He also poisoned the tea of a whole ward; nevertheless, a psychiatrist thought that he had so far reformed that he could safely be released. (The psychiatrists who examined Young when he was fourteen said that they thought he would remain a menace for the rest of his life.)

But Graham Young was released; no one was informed of his previous history in order that there should be no prejudice against him and he should not suffer from the stigma of having been in Broadmoor. He quickly found a job working in a company manufacturing high-grade photographic equipment where, helping with the distribution of the tea, he soon poisoned several of the company's employees with thallium, two of them dying in the most horrible agony. They were the first murders committed with thallium in Britain; it is uncertain whether Young had read and was inspired by Agatha Christie's novel in which the victim is murdered with thallium. At first, the deaths and illness among the staff were attributed to a mysterious virus; it was Young's public boastfulness of his knowledge of heavy-metal poisoning that led to the true diagnosis and his conviction. (One of his victims, in the meantime, had been cremated. It was the first time in British legal history that a murder was proved by the chemical analysis of ashes.)

Several aspects of the case intrigue me. Young was very intelligent but he never had the staying-power, the necessary humility or the discipline necessary to achieve real mastery of a subject. Wanting fame, and unable to separate it from notoriety, resorted to disreputable or criminal means to achieve it. It was his declared aim to become the greatest poisoner since Palmer.

I once met a prisoner whose desire for fame exceeded his capacity to obtain it in a constructive way. He was intelligent, but not quite intelligent enough. He therefore set himself the goal of becoming the most difficult and notorious prisoner in the English prison system; and even if there are so many types of difficulty that it is impossible to say who is the most difficult, he certainly succeeded in being sufficiently difficult that he was rotated round the prisons of the country, changing every two weeks in order that each prison should take its share, but no more than its share, of the burden. In a world that worships celebrity – only just in formation in Young's poisoning days – the need to distinguish yourself from others seems more important than ever before, and the means by which you do so less important than ever before. Where Palmer poisoned for money, Young did like for fame.

Young was intelligent, but he was also better educated than he would have been today. His letter of application for a job was far better written than anyone with the same number of years of schooling as he would be able to write today. When he testified in his own defence at his own trial in 1970, he showed powers of expression and analytical thought that were a tribute not only to his native wit, but to the education that he had received. (This suggests that education in the formal sense is not in every case accompanied by high moral development.)

One's impression that the formal education of the time was better than it is today is only strengthened by a memoir, published in 1973, by his elder sister, Winifred (whom he tried to poison), called *Obsessive Poisoner: The Strange Case of Graham Young*. Winifred had no tertiary education, and went on to be a secretary, but her book is extremely well-written, its prose limpid and its narrative technique exemplary. In short, it is highly literate, of a standard that nineteen out of twenty graduates today could not equal. One does not know, of course, how much editing it required; but one also knows, from experience, that one cannot make a silk purse out of a sow's ear.

There is an aspect of the book that is more important still from the philosophical point of view. I do not think anyone could read it without being struck by the sheer decency, the unselfconscious goodness, of the author. Her struggle to retain some affection for her brother, despite his having tried to poison her for the sheer pleasure of doing so, her evident lack of bitterness or resentment towards him or anyone else, her unassuming moral poise and equilibrium, are truly impressive and restore one's faith in the possibility of human decency, in the sense that George Orwell gave to that word.

But it is not only Winifred Young who was good.

Graham Young certainly did not emerge from a sink of iniquity, from a swamp of asocial egotism, as one expects psychopaths nowadays to do. On the contrary, all his relatives were good, kind, decent people. His mother died soon after his birth of tuberculosis, far sooner than could have given rise to any psychological trauma that might explain, or rather be used to explain, his subsequent behaviour. But his stepmother, whom almost certainly he murdered, was a good person too. His father, whom he also tried to poison, was an honest, upstanding man who took his responsibilities to his children seriously, and of whom no serious ill is known.

Graham Young manifested his strangeness very early in his life. Nothing in his background or upbringing explains it. One is forced, therefore, to conclude that he was congenitally abnormal; that he was born with a deficient makeup that rendered him, in H.C. Prichard's sense, morally insane.

This, of course, gives rise to difficult questions, the kind of questions that philosophers have been wrestling with ever since the days of Socrates without having found definitive answers to them. (How disappointing it would be to them if the answers were found – what would there be left for philosophers to do?)

If Graham Young were congenitally liable to commit evil by some quirk of birth, genetic or otherwise, how are we to evaluate him morally? Even if we claim to be completely consequentialist in our morality – that we consider an act good or bad solely according to the consequences it has – we very seldom are in reality, because it is psychologically impossible for human beings to be consequentialist in their morality, either about acts or about men. We normally consider a man bad not only because his acts have bad consequences, but because he has bad motives and knowingly does what is wrong. An act with unanticipated good consequences, but done from the worst motives, remains a bad act; and the man who performs such an act is a bad man, at least if his bad act is not merely, as murderers often call their crimes, 'a one-off.'

Graham Young was a compulsive poisoner (*Compulsive Poisoner* would have been a better title than *Obsessive Poisoner* for Winifred Young's book). We know that he was a compulsive poisoner because he used every available opportunity to poison people, irrespective of the consequences to himself, and for no gain other than the satisfaction of having performed the act itself. And why did he use every available opportunity to poison people? Because he was a compulsive poisoner, of course, and that is what compulsive poisoners do.

I have heard this kind of circular argument put forward in court by expert witnesses, much to the delight of the cross-examining barrister who is soon able to make it (the argument) and them (the expert witnesses) look empty and ridiculous. The *explicandum* (that which is to be explained) is indistinguishable from the *explicans* (the explanation), so nothing is explained at all; and the expert becomes but a sounding brass and a tinkling cymbal.

Oddly enough, it is only to very bad acts that we apply this circular thinking, as though only very bad acts, and not good ones, were anomalous.

Graham Young's badness requires explanation, but not Winifred's goodness. Likewise, we search for explanations for our bad behaviour, but not for our good, which is purely the result of the rightful exercise of free choice and therefore reflects well on us in a way that bad behaviour does not reflect ill.

From the delightful labyrinth of moral philosophy there is no exit. He who enters it never leaves, at any rate not with the prize that he is seeking. Perhaps people like Graham Young are fascinating (in part) because they are the most sensational stress-tests of our moral philosophy.

My copy of Anthony Holden's book about Graham Young bears the bookplate of W. Gregg. This bookplate might alarm the average reader, for it is quartered thus:

```
                    E
                    X

                    L
                    I
                    B
                    R
                    I
                    S

                    E
                    X
EX LIBRIS EX LIBRIS EX LIBRIS
                    I
                    B
                    R
                    I
                    S

                    E
                    X

                    L
                    I
                    B
                    R
                    I
                    S
```

In the top left hand quarter are some bars in the wall of a prison cell; in the top right hand quarter a guillotine. In the bottom left hand quarter is a scaffold and rope; in the bottom right hand corner an electric chair.

From this, one might be inclined to suppose that W. Gregg was a morbid man with sadistic tendencies. But Wilfred Gregg was neither. He was a quiet, dutiful, modest man who worked for thirty-seven years before retirement as a civil servant, in the meantime building up his collection of books about murder, nearly 7000 of them by the time of his death aged seventy-six, which he housed in an extension to his suburban bungalow. One bookseller who sometimes supplies me with books about crime (in which he has specialised for forty years) told me that he was a gentle soul, polite and kindly. After his retirement, he wrote (or compiled) *An Encyclopaedia of Mass Murder* and *An Encyclopaedia of Serial Murder*. Apart from murder, he loved bulldogs.

His library, almost sixty years in the making, was dispersed after his death. His wife died before him, and the marriage was, as it used to say in obituaries, 'without issue.' Many of his books were no doubt rare enough, but not so rare that any institutional library of any scale would not already have them, and so none wanted to buy it as a collection. (With the exception of a few items, the same could be said of my library and, solid as it seems to me now, it will share the fate of Wilfred Gregg's.)

9

Free Hands

I had bought in Dublin, cheaply as I thought, a first edition of Samuel Johnson's *Lives of the Most Eminent English Poets*, and noticed throughout the four volumes annotations or additions in eighteenth-century writing in brown-discoloured ink (at least, I assumed that the brown colour was a discoloration). At first I assumed that these annotations were the work of an agitated pedant, eager to prove his superiority over the great Cham by correcting his errors.

But there was something too measured about them, too scholarly, without the expostulations of disgust, outrage, contempt or all the other delightful emotions (that is to say, emotions that give delight to those who experience them) that annotators of books usually express. The handwriting, moreover, was steady, and displayed no obvious tendency to shake with excitement at the discovery of the error of so eminent a man.

It was Valerie Meyers, the wife of Geoffrey Meyers, the literary biographer and scholar – and herself a literary scholar of great accomplishment – both of whom were staying at my house that – in my mind at any rate – is but a dormitory annexe to my library, who found a part of the solution. She suggested that I compare the annotations with a subsequent edition of the *Lives*, and lo and behold the annotations exactly corresponded to the changes from the first edition.

It is strange how this discovery excited me, to the point of causing my hand to tremble: I who in my early adulthood had sought out danger like a long-lost friend, and travelled with smugglers, interviewed political murderers, and braved the attention of more than one secret service. That it should come to this! As the Germans say, every little animal has its little pleasure. If I am to be perfectly honest, my cupidity was excited too.

Could it be that I held in my hand the book that Doctor Johnson himself held while correcting the first edition of his *Lives*, published three years before his death? The handwriting itself was too steady to be his, he who was short-sighted and given to nervous tics, and moreover afflicted with a variety of the illnesses of old age. But perhaps it was the writing of an amanuensis, taking dictation from him.

I am neither a Johnson scholar nor a detective, but my mind began to roam over the possibilities. I bought the volumes in Dublin, so perhaps the amanuensis was an Irishman. Yes, that was it, Edmund Malone! After all, he was a friend of Johnson's, and annotated four editions of Boswell's biography. These, then, were the books from which Edmond Malone took down dictation from Samuel Johnson! QED.

Is it better to live in a fool's paradise – the only kind there is, actually – than to face hard reality? On my wall is a fine early eighteenth-century portrait of John Gay, author of *The Beggar's Opera*, that I believe is in the style of Hogarth, but I dare not take to Christies in case it should turn out to be – in their opinion – the work of a mere journeyman, a copy or a fake. I prefer to preserve intact my dream that I have made a coup, thanks to my superior powers of discrimination, by having bought the picture cheap.

I found the solution to the Johnson puzzle on the back of a letter in the middle of the fourth volume of the *Lives*. This solution was interesting enough from the point of view of literary history, but not such as would render me rich, even in theory (I would never have sold a valuable book in any case, at least not until my situation was desperate). The letter was that of a distinguished philosophy don at Trinity College, David Berman, to the editor of *The Scriblerian*, a journal dedicated to the study of eighteenthcentury British writers, regarding an article he had written for it. It was on the back of this letter that I found the complete solution to the mystery, written in the fine hand of a true scholar:

> Boswell's *Life of Johnson*
> (Oxford 1934) vol. IV, p. 63 n.
> Mr Chalmers here records a curious literary anecdote – that when a new & enlarged edition of the *Lives of the Poets* were (sic) published in 1783, Mr. Nichols, in justice to the purchasers of the preceding edition, printed the additions in a separate pamphlet, and advertised that it might be had *gratis*. Not ten copies were called for. Croker, 1831.

In fact, this pamphlet was unlikely to be the source of the emendations (the British Library does not possess a copy of it). Professor Berman, obviously a man of deep erudition, goes on to quote Courtney and Smith's bibliography of Johnson, in the 1925 edition, to the effect that most of the corrections were printed in the *London Magazine* for September, 1783, p142, and that of the pamphlet 'scarcely a single copy was demanded.' My hopes were dashed, my hand gave up its tremble.

There was one compensation, however (apart from renewed steadiness of the hand), for my disappointment. I had envisaged myself scouring libraries to find examples of Edmund Malone's handwriting to compare with that in my copy of the *Lives*. At least this would no longer be necessary. What I also did not know at the time of my excitement was that Malone's handwriting was notoriously bad and difficult to decipher. The writing in my copy of the *Lives* was legible and even elegant. These two facts alone might have told me that I was contemplating a wild-goose chase, had I but known both of them.

10

Pools Full of Water

What is written in books is not of interest in proportion to the prominence or fame of the person who writes it, however, very far from that. Sometimes I find moving inscriptions by untraceable or even unnamed persons, in otherwise ordinary books.

An inscription that never fails to give me a slight lump in the throat, or even brings tears to my eyes, is a very simple one. It is in the first commercial edition of Cyril Connolly's *The Unquiet Grave*, published in 1945. The inscription, in a cultivated hand though the ink is beginning to run out by the end of it, is in three lines:

> To my beloved husband
> Christmas 1945
> R.J. Watson

Why does something so simple, not to say ordinary and even banal, have so enduring and powerful an effect on me?

First, of course, is the melancholy of the passage of time – not of aeons, for the passage of aeons has no emotional impact, it means no more to us than distances measured in light-years – but of a period that can be encompassed and comprehended within a single life-time. My guess is that R.J. Watson was not very old when she wrote the inscription, let us say around 30, in which case she would be a nonagenarian now. This thought is melancholy enough: the implacability of time's arrow, the fleetingness of youth, the inevitability of aging. If R.J. Watson, whom I always imagine whenever I open this book as a beautiful young woman of intelligent yet gentle mien with waving flaxen hair, in a sweater, pearl earrings and an elegant tweed skirt, is alive still, she probably sits all day up against the wall of the day room of a nursing home, perhaps not all there in her mind, surrounded by the smell of incontinence and the cry of the demented.

I suspect, even worse, that both R.J. Watson and her beloved husband have passed away, to use our current euphemism for being dead. For is it conceivable that anyone who inscribed a book thus, or was the recipient of such an inscription, should disembarrass him or herself of the book (which is so slender that it couldn't encumber a room the size of a coffin) before death? I think not; it was via the children, or perhaps less close relatives, that the book found its way into the shop where I bought it.

Is it not strange that the melancholy thoughts about the inexorable march of time and life itself that such a book evokes should be in some way also pleasurable, or at least consolatory?

It is the same consolation that I derive from visiting graveyards and cemeteries, 'where the rude forefathers of the hamlet sleep,' that I do (just as I always enter second-hand bookshops) if I have the slightest chance. Many a contented afternoon have I spent among the tombs, reading the names and dates; I love the old formulae, such as 'Here lies John Smith, Grocer of this Town, *also* Abigail his wife.'

The tombs that most move me are those that are not so

ancient, but were erected relatively recently, say within the lifetime of my own parents. How powerful are the mute stories that they tell, with all the implications of the fact that a woman followed her husband, or a man his wife, into the grave thirty-five years after he or she died! Years of loneliness, years of fidelity to memory. Sometimes one comes across the tomb of an infant, died aged three months sixty-five years ago, with fresh flowers recently left by it. The parents, now in their late eighties at least, have not forgotten him; perhaps they were unable to have another child. I imagine them: their dignity as great as their grief is deep.

Not long ago a graveyard, or at least a scene in a grave-yard, restored my faith, never very strong and always rather fragile, in the possibility of human goodness. It was in Llanelli, in South Wales, an unlovely town blessed, howev-er, with at least two nice cemeteries (the writer Rhys Davies said that the Welsh were fond of a good funeral, and a decent burial was for them the precondition – or is it the post-condition? – of having had a good life).

It being a fine day, I had gone to read in the graveyard of an old church and there was approached by a Muslim woman in Pakistani dress, clutching a bouquet, who spoke good enough but strongly accented English. She asked me whether I knew where was the grave of someone with a common Welsh name (Margaret Davies, I seem to remem-ber). The woman who asked me had lived in Llanelli years ago, and Margaret Davies had been her next-door neigh-bour then. Margaret had died in the meantime and now that she, the Pakistani lady, was passing through Llanelli again, she wanted to put flowers on her grave.

I was very touched. Here was evidence of the possibility of sympathy and understanding between two people of very different culture and experience. Of course, it is one of the teachings of literature that human understanding (as well as its opposite, incomprehension) is possible in difficult circumstances; but it is nevertheless reassuring to have a practical confirmation of it. And it seemed to me also very unlikely that such understanding or sympathy would have developed between them without goodness on both sides of the relationship.

Notwithstanding the subtle joys of melancholy induced by the inscription in my copy of *The Unquiet Grave*, the reason that it – the inscription – was and is so precious to me, so painful and yet so cathartic, acting as does the wounded surgeon who plies the steel that questions the distempered part, is even much personal.

It seems to me that the simplicity of the inscription is almost a guarantee, or at any rate evidence much in favour, of its sincerity: its absolute truth.

Who, reading it, could doubt that R.J. Watson loved her husband? Had there been any doubt of it, had she been an hysteric, say, or someone trying to persuade herself that she felt more than she really did feel, her words would have been more emphatic, her dedication more rococo. But:

> They are not empty hearted
> Whose words reverb no hollowness.

Even the way she signs her name, R.J. Watson, persuades me of this. Of course, little terms of endearment, often known to be such only to the people using or receiving them, can be a sign of deep affection; but they can also be the paper that hides the cracks.

No woman affixes her name R.J. Watson to a document destined for her husband unless she loves him passionately or is about to divorce him (not that passionate love is incompatible with divorce either). As it happens, I noticed early in my career as a doctor that informality of address between husbands and wives could mean anything at all; but formality – as when a man called his wife Mrs Smith and she called him Mr Smith – invariably meant a successful marriage and an unbreakable bond.

The love in this inscription is evident, and it breaks my heart: for I am convinced that love is one of the very few things in life worth having or giving, but also – alas! – I know that I have had severe difficulties in this regard all my life. Passionately affectionate by nature, I had all expressiveness squeezed out of me as a child. What is not given with generosity is not received with grace, and what is received without grace rarely continues to be given with generosity.

Even now, affection embarrasses me, not the thing itself but the expression of it, physical or verbal as the case may be. Many are the people for whom I would gladly and unhesitatingly lay down my life; but not for anything would I hug them, or express any feeling for them. As to the suggestion that I should be able to overcome my little difficulty, because I have some inkling from whence it came, I can only refer him who makes it to Sonnet 129:

All this the world well knows; yet none knows well
To shun the heaven that leads men to this hell.

Of course, Shakespeare was speaking of lust, not of the lower grades of human passion, such as mere affection; but that knowledge of the origin of any undesirable characteristic – an apparent coldness of heart in my case – is equivalent to overcoming it, and replacing it by something better is, I am afraid, a shallow modern superstition.

Freud, who was perhaps the most important originator of this superstition, even if he did not intend to be so, once wrote that if a man has been his mother's undisputed darling he retains throughout life the triumphant feeling, the confidence in success. I think the opposite might also be true: if a passionate child is rejected, he retains a fear of a repetition for the rest of his life, and avoids that dreadful possibility by constructing a carapace for himself. Fortunately, however, I have been able to compensate in other directions, so that on the whole I have had an interesting and even an amusing life. As the book of Common Prayer puts it: Blessed is the man… who going through the vale of misery, use it for a well: and the pools are full of water.

So I both admire and envy R.J. Watson her ability and willingness freely and vulnerably to expose herself to another, the price of the greatest happiness known to man. We of course only admire those whom we cannot fully become ourselves (or at any rate, ought only to admire such as they, for otherwise we are on the slippery slope to self-admiration). I admire R.J. Watson because she could express what I would find it easier to write in a book than to express in spoken words. The fact that the Christmas gift is a small one, nothing extravagant, a very slim volume, only adds to my admiration of her: no grand gestures, only unmistakable, undiluted love.

11

Glaring Light

As to Cyril Connolly's book itself, *The Unquiet Grave*, it seems to me undisciplined and self-indulgent (but that may be the pot calling the kettle black), a series of laments and rationalisations of his failure to do what the very first sentence of the book claims is the only true function of a writer:

> The more books we read, the sooner we perceive that the true function of the writer is to produce a masterpiece and that no other task is of any consequence.

Of this I am not sure, or rather, I am sure that it is not so. A library that had nothing but masterpieces on its shelves would be tedious, and very soon wear us out; and if we had never had access to any other library, or worse still if no other library existed, we should not even know that the books on its shelves were masterpieces.

All judgment, said Dr Johnson, is comparative; and thus we authors of lesser works are performing a task of the utmost and inestimable importance, for they permit readers to recognise a masterpiece when they read it. Without us, then, there would be no masterpieces. We create masterpieces indirectly.

In his *Rambler* essay number 145, for August 6, 1751, entitled 'Petty writers not to be despised,' the great man comes to our defence:

> The *ephemerae* of learning have uses more ade-
> quate to the purposes of common life than more
> pompous and more durable volumes... Every
> size of readers requires a genius of correspon-
> dent capacity; some delight in abstracts and epit-
> omes, because they want room in their memory
> for long details, and content themselves with
> effects, without enquiry after causes; some
> minds are overpowered by splendour of senti-
> ment, as some eyes are offended by the glaring
> light...

Moreover – though Johnson does not say it – our minds are not all of a piece as far as inclination is concerned. I can read Aristotle for an hour, but not all day; I can read Agatha Christie in bed, but not at ten in the morning. Connolly is talking bunk of the kind that high-minded aesthetes often talk.

At one point, quite late in the book, Connolly quotes (without translation, no monoglots need read *him*) Sainte-Beuve, a quotation that has particular resonance for me:

> *Je ne suis pas complètement moi que la plume en main et*
> *dans le silence du cabinet.*
> (I am only completely myself pen in hand and in
> the silence of the study.)

There is something deeply mutilated about this (though it describes me well enough), for is not man supposed to be a

social animal who lives and takes his being by serving and
being served by others? But there are compensations for the
mutilated man to whom writing is, if not everything, at least
the main meaning of his existence. (I have often wondered
what became of writers before the invention of writing and
even more of printing.)

A man to whom writing is so important looks at life as
though it were an aquarium, and he outside looking in. Once,
for example, I was arrested in Albania (naturally on a visit
after democracy had been instituted – I cannot, in this context, say restored). I had gone into the main square,
Skanderbeg, of Tirana, to take photographs of the police,
who a few months before had been loyal communists dedicated to upholding the regime, violently dispersing a demonstration against the current government by a small crowd of –
communists. It so happened that this demonstration occurred
on the morning of the day of my departure.

While I was taking my snaps of people running away from
a rain of truncheon blows, I felt my upper arm suddenly
gripped as if by iron. It was, in fact, the grip of a large policeman, against whom it would have been folly to struggle. He
pulled me towards a vehicle of the kind that is used to round
up stray dogs, and threw me into it as if I weighed nothing,
administering a few smart blows with his truncheon *en route*.
My only protest against this high-handed treatment was the
following exclamation:

'You can't arrest me, I have a plane to catch!'

Luckily he spoke no English, for the outward modesty
of my demeanour notwithstanding, this exclamation
revealed the arrogance and self-importance within me
that is always struggling to get out, like the furies in

Pandora's Box, and sometimes does.

Three Albanians, one of whom spoke perfect English, were likewise thrown into the caged vehicle, and then we were driven off helter-skelter through the streets to a police station, where we were hauled out and encouraged not to dawdle by a few more blows of the truncheon. We were thrown into the same cell.

A suspect was being interrogated, or made to confess, a few cells away. He was screaming with pain as several policemen kicked and beat him, and shouted abuse and threats at him. The Albanians with whom I was incarcerated began to scream and shout and wail themselves, whereupon I decided to take charge. I ordered the man who spoke English to translate.

'Tell them to stop it,' I said, 'or they'll get us all beaten. This is no time to be Balkan; they'll have to start being British. Britons do not make a fuss. They do not shout or scream or cry. Tell them to be quiet and dignified.'

Oddly enough it worked. Perhaps it was the realisation that I was right, or the effect of the shock of being in the company of someone as peculiar as I, but they desisted at once, as cicadas stop chirping at dusk. Of course, I felt a slight pang of conscience at what I said, for it was not true. It might once have been true that Britons did not make a fuss, that they did not shout, scream or cry, though torture might, perhaps, have been regarded as an extenuating circumstance for it if they did, but it was not true now. Still, a little lie, containing an element of nostalgia for my lost countrymen, seemed permissible in the circumstances, even though Kant would not have permitted it. Even at such a strange moment, the opinion of Kant was present in my mind?

> Truthfulness… is the formal duty of an individ-
> ual to everyone, however great the disadvantages
> to himself or to another.

Then came a moral crisis, and I cannot say to this day whether
I passed the test or not. I incline to the negative.

Friends of mine had witnessed my arrest and contacted
the high government official with whom, as it happens, we
had dined the night before. He ordered my release.

When the policeman who had struck me came to the cell
and beckoned for me to leave, I did not know, but strongly
suspected, that this was what had happened. The policeman's
attitude towards me was now distinctly sheepish, and I
realised that there had been a decisive change in the balance
of power between us. His fate, or at any rate his career, was in
my hands and I could revenge myself upon him if I so
wished, or so he must have thought. I had no desire for
vengeance. However; the question was, should I agree to go
from the cell, leaving my three co-detainees to their fate?

I went, telling myself I should be more use to them at liberty than still in the cell. But of course this reasoning also
coincided with what I wanted to do, a very convenient coincidence. If I am truthful, I was more concerned to catch my
plane (which I did). True, I made representations on their
behalf through a friend and they were released; but I did not
stay until they were released. As Hamlet puts it:

> A thought which, quarter'd, hath but one part wisdom
> And ever three parts coward.

On my way out of the police station, to be chauffeured back to my hotel in the best car available, the policeman who had struck me put his right hand over his heart and bowed slightly to me, in a gesture of deep repentance that he had hit someone connected to the powerful. Ever since, no doubt irrationally (it is called in psychology 'one-trial learning'), I have felt a deep and visceral repugnance for hands on hearts – not that I was very keen on them before.

Though I was deeply involved in the episode, I was also completely detached from it, as if I were an observer rather than a participant, and anthropologist come among torturers. At every moment, even while being hit, I was thinking, 'How am I going to describe this?' The policeman was beating me, and I was thinking of the right word. If he had known this, no doubt he would have tried a bit harder.

Now it is an excellent thing to be able to detach yourself from your experience in this fashion; it makes what is boring interesting and what is painful bearable (within limits). It reduces suffering – your own at any rate. But like most excellent things, a surfeit can be bad for you. It is habit-forming, and then you go through life as if it were a charade mounted for your entertainment, or to provide you with material. People become insects to you, buzzing around. People notice that you are disconnected from them and are offended by it. The notebook, the search for the apt phrase, comes between you and genuine feeling. And you even become an object to yourself.

Doctors, no doubt, are particularly prone to this psychological deformation. They see every permutation of human

suffering (or at least they used to in Britain, until the imple-
mentation of the European Working Time Directive). But
they are trained not to respond to such suffering in the way
natural to the sympathetic layman. They used, in the days
before most reality became virtual, to be sent into the dissect-
ing room on their first day in medical school, precisely to learn
to control their natural emotions, in this case repugnance, for
some greater end, in this case passing anatomy exams. After all,
a doctor who broke down every time he encountered something tragic or horrible would be about as much use as a grief
counsellor in a nuclear war (or after someone's death, come to
that).

A Somerset Maugham, who thought that his training as a
doctor stood him in excellent stead as a writer though he never
actually practised after qualification, put much of himself and
his philosophy (as he would like them to have been rather than
as they really, at a deeper level, were), into the protagonist, Dr
Saunders, of his novel *The Narrow Corner*.:

> Dr Saunders took an interest in his fellows that
> was not quite scientific and not quite human. He
> wanted to receive entertainment from them. He
> regarded them dispassionately and it gave him
> just the same amusement to unravel the intrica-
> cies of the individual as a mathematician might
> find in the solution of a problem... He was very
> easy to get on with. But he had no friends. He
> was an agreeable companion, but neither sought
> intimacy nor gave it. There was no one in the
> world to whom he was not at heart indifferent.
>
> He was selfish, but since he was at the same

time shrewd and disinterested, few knew it and none was inconvenienced by it. He confounded persons and patients. Each was like another page in an interminable book, and that there were so many repetitions added oddly to the interest. It was curious to see how all these people responded to the critical situations of humanity, but the sight neither touched his heart nor troubled his nerves. He felt neither sorrow nor pity. And yet his manner was full of sympathy. It could not be denied that he had led a good life, for he was charitable and kindly, and he devoted his energies to the alleviation of pain, but if motive counts for righteousness, then he served no praise; for he was influenced in his actions neither by love, pity, nor charity.

This is not many steps removed from Buddhism, with its belief that the elimination of pain is the highest good, and that since all desire inevitably leads to pain (*post coitum omne animal triste* – every animal is sad after coitus), pleasure must be eliminated as well. It is not a coincidence that Maugham wrote extensively about the East, and set several novels and stories about the search for spiritual peace there, he had so many sources of unhappiness that the life of Dr Saunders, whom on occasion he outwardly resembled, must have seemed to him ideal.

At times to me too. The chair in my library, however, is a halfway house between attachment and detachment, between the sacred Bo-tree and the world at large.

12

A White Van

Travelling through Central America, I was driving a white
Toyota pick-up truck. I was writing a book about Guatemala
at the time, but wanted also to see El Salvador, Honduras
and Nicaragua (Costa Rica interested me less because there
was no civil war). I had spent some time in El Salvador, then,
like Guatemala, in the throes of a civil war. In San Salvador,
its capital, customers of supermarkets were asked to leave
their guns outside in containers that in other countries might
have served as umbrella stands but were here filled with
automatic weapons. It was not difficult to recognise the cars
of the death-squads, with the blacked-out out windows with
a small round area of clear glass for the drivers to peer out
of. In Guatemala, by contrast, it was the *panel blanco* – the
white van – of which one had to be wary.

The President of El Salvador at the time was a Christian
Democrat called Napoleon Duarte, who had himself been
the victim of torture by a military regime. He was now the
democratic face, or facade, of a still-highly militarised state
that was fighting a guerrilla insurgency led by intellectuals. A
Salvadoran peasant said to me something that I have never
forgotten, for it seemed to me to indicate a very
sophisticated understanding.

'The guerrillas are better men than the soldiers,' he said,
'but I don't want them to win.'

Duarte was known by journalists as *Old Leatherlungs*, on account of his ability to speak for hours at press conferences without pause (in fact, he was mortally ill, and died soon after of lung cancer). He was generally despised by all right-thinking people, that is to say all foreigners favourable to the guerrillas. I was not one of them: the press was much freer under his rule than it had been before, despite the fact that guerrillas still often lobbed grenades into the centre of the city after nightfall and the American embassy was covered in rocket-repellent netting.

The largest bookshop in San Salvador was called *La Catedral del Libro*, the Cathedral of the Book. It had an impressive stock. On the same table, for example, were piles of *Mi lucha*, by Adolfo Hitler, and of *El Capital* by Carlos Marx, separated by another of *Cafemáncia* (the art of telling the future from coffee grounds), whose author I do not recall.

I bought a large supply of books about El Salvador at *La Catedral*, including one about Rutilio Grande, a priest who (as was fashionable among priests at the time) supported the guerrillas, joined them and lost his life. It was this little book, among others, that got me into trouble at the Honduran border.

When I arrived at the border post, the Honduran border guard found the books, about thirty of them, in the back of my truck. He was at once very suspicious, and thought I must be a dangerous character. He took Rutilio Grande, and one or two others, to his boss, who concluded that I ought to be deported without delay.

I had quite forgotten that in any case the Hondurans hated Salvadorans and all their works, and that for a foreigner to express a sympathetic interest in the history and politics of El

Salvador might not necessarily recommend him very highly to Hondurans. This was despite having read a book a few years previously (and which I still possess, as I never dispose of a book) about the so-called soccer war between El Salvador and Honduras that erupted over a disputed penalty kick in a game between the two countries, in which three thousand people were killed and tens of thousands were forced to flee their homes. The author of the book, an American anthropologist, refused to believe that a war could 'really' be about something as trivial as a penalty kick, and proved to his own satisfaction that, on the contrary, it was 'really' about land for subsistence farming, El Salvador being a very overcrowded country whose population suffered from land hunger, and Honduras being unpopulated with much uncultivated land.

What does 'really' mean in this context? When I bought and read the book, the hypothesis of human foolishness appealed to me much more as an explanation than the economic interpretation. I was anxious to reassure myself as my life was drifting and aimless at the time thanks to deficiencies in my character, that I was not remotely as foolish as it is possible for humans to be. (One of my favourite titles on my shelves is *A Brief Introduction to the History of Human Stupidity*, by Walter B. Pitkin, published in 1936 – since when, of course, stupidity has not been on the wane, despite the fact that the book was translated into fifteen languages. The brief introduction is 547 pages long. Another of the author's books is *Life Begins at 40*.)

Here in defence of my preference for the argument from stupidity I could point out that, forty years later, Egypt and Algeria might well have gone to war over a very similar incident if they had happened to share a border as El Salvador and Honduras had done. I cannot help but recall this when, for some reason, I received by e-mail the United Nations Development Programme's press releases for its Sport for Development programme, e-mails that allege that international sport fosters not only economic development but also understanding between nations.

I was deported from Honduras at my own expense. I had to pay for a soldier to accompany me to the Nicaraguan border. He obviously did not consider me a very dangerous type, because we had no sooner set out than he fell fast asleep, his gun held between his sleeping knees with its barrel pointing directly at my head. I was hoping that he had put the safety catch on, for the road was full of potholes; I never discovered whether or not he had done so, but I did survive. His powers of sleep were formidable and he woke only for lunch, which I bought him.

The only other time in my life I was arrested (and deported) was there. In Nicaragua, I soon acquired a relatively formidable little library of contemporary Nicaraguan publications. They were exceedingly cheap because they were state produced, heavily subsidised and all written from the same point of view, namely that of the government's mixture of anti-American nationalism and self-congratulatory socialism, which it wished to instil in the population at the expense of all other ways of thinking. There was an outpouring of revolutionary historiography, establishing that the present government, the Sandinista, was both an inevitable denouement of all Nicaraguan history hitherto, and at the same time morally beyond reproach.

Anyone familiar, as I was, with this genre as produced in Cuba would at once recognise the pattern, and I bought many of the books not because they were interesting in themselves – once you had read one, you had in essence read them all – but because they seemed to me a documentary record of an important historical moment (whose importance has now faded somewhat). I doubted that there would be copies of this literature in any British library, and intended one day to donate them to a library with an interest in Latin America.

There was also an outpouring of poetry after the revolution, or at least an outpouring of publication of poetry (I once read that three quarters of British youth, not generally very poetic either in appearance or conduct, wrote poetry at one time or other), that was mostly abominable, lacking form, vehement rather than feeling, and as stale and stereotyped in imagery as in that used by a management consultant. There was one exception, the priest-poet-politician, Ernesto Cardenal, whose poetry had real merit (though he was a very good poet well before the revolution).

I committed to memory, from which it has since escaped, his poem, *Somoza desveliza la estatua de Somoza en el Estadio Somoza*, Somoza Unveils a Statue of Somoza in the Somoza Stadium, a title that alone perfectly captures the absurdity and preposterousness of dictatorship. In Paraguay I once arrived in Puerto Stroessner aboard the *MV Alfredo Stroessner* while the *Polka Alfredo Stroessner* (one of a collection of songs on a record entitled *Cantos a mi general*, Songs for My General) was played over the public address system.

A truck-load of books and revolutionary pamphlets from

Nicaragua might well have caused me some difficulty at the borders of El Salvador and Guatemala when I returned to those countries: countries that were, after all, fighting Marxist insurgencies of their own, and whose border guards could hardly have been expected to distinguish between ironists such as I, who mistrusted the revolutionaries, and the fellow-travellers of the revolutionaries, as most foreign visitors in those days were.

In the event, no one took the slightest notice of the incriminating literature, not even of a copy of the cyclostyled warning by the *Frente Farabundo Martí para le Liberación Nacional* (FMLN) to the *alcalde* (mayor) of a town in El Salvador, that he would be killed if he participated in the forthcoming elections, and that I preserved as a souvenir of the times. Apart from the actual menace of death, it was couched in the most chivalrous terms of almost rococo elaboration and politeness: one could almost imagine it being used as a model in one of those books to teach people the correct form of letters, under the heading 'Threatening a mayor with death during an election,' which comes immediately after 'Thanking a bishop for having opened garden party.'

Strangely enough, it was while I was writing about my trouble at the Honduran border that another incident involving a book and a border returned to my memory. I was on a train from Lourenço Marques, as it was then still called, in newly-independent Mozambique, to Johannesburg. Suffice it to say that this was not much of a tourist route at the time, indeed I was the only passenger on board, political tensions being high to say the least. I was quite clearly regarded by the train's guard as something of a lunatic.

I had a few books with me that (thanks to the difference

between the official and black- or open-market, rate of exchange) I had bought for fractions of a single penny at the English club in Beira, to which English-speaking tourists from Rhodesia and South Africa had once gone as a coastal resort. But the book that aroused the Afrikaner border policeman's suspicion was the Oxford Standard Author's Shakespeare I had with me printed on India paper. He flicked through it and then said:

'Are these *all* the plays of Shakespeare?'

He managed by his intonation to imply that there was something very sinister in the possibility that I had deliberately excluded certain of the Bard's works – by cutting them out, perhaps – from the volume. I said what I then believed, that they were all the works, though I have since learned that some authorities now ascribe other plays to him as well. But it was clear from the policeman's manner that he mistrusted deeply readers as a class.

Actually, I have some sympathy with this view. Readers can be very unreliable, even dangerous.

13

The Present State

I bought my copy of Rex Warner's *The Wild Goose Chase* (knowing him to be only a very moderate novelist, if an excellent translator from the Greek) because of the inscription, or rather two inscriptions in a cultured hand:

> Bought at Portmadoc and read while on holiday
> at Portmeirion 10 x 1947

The second inscription, dated thirty years and nine days later, in a hand that had not changed at all, despite the probability that the writer was now very old himself, written with the same pen and the same ink (something that would be unthinkable now), said:

> The last book read by Barbara during the illness
> which ended in her death. She liked the book
> enormously 19 x 1977

This, too, seizes my heart, both with sadness and a strange, indefinable consolation for that sadness. There is irony, too, for the first sentence of *The Wild Goose Chase* runs as follows:

> I continually wonder how I may account for my
> present state, which, I suppose, it would be accu-

rate to describe as one of death.

I remember much of 1977 as if it were yesterday. I went off to India with the intention of not coming back for months, perhaps for years, perhaps ever, seeking material for a great book. Instead, I suffered from a viral illness on the plane to Delhi, developed viral myocarditis and went into heart failure, from which, I suppose, I might have died (there's karma for you). I recovered and returned to England to resume my career, such as it was, after a brief stay in hospital during which nothing was discovered about my illness that was not known already.

Camus famously said that there is only one really serious philosophical problem, that of suicide, but he was wrong: the only really serious philosophical problem is that of death, and what it means for life. I once bought another book for its anonymous inscription, though I was also mildly interested in the book's subject-matter also, as who could not be? Dated 1816, by Joseph Taylor, its title could hardly be accused of lack of specificity about the contents:

> The Danger of Premature Interment, Proved from Many Remarkable Instances of People who have recovered after being laid out for dead, and of others entombed alive, for want of being properly examined prior to Interment. Also a Description of the Manner the Ancient Egyptians, and other Nations, Preserved and

Venerated their Dead, and a curious Account of
their Sepulchral Ever Burning Lamps and
Mausoleums. Likewise the pernicious effects of
burying in the body of Churches, and confined
Church-Yards pointed out, whereby many valuable lives have been lost, to the Public, and their
Friends, Selected from Historical Records.

Underneath the name of the author, in small italic letters in
inverted commas, is what appears to be a quotation, whose
source I have not even tried to trace:

'To revive nailed up in a Coffin! A return of Life
in Darkness, Distraction and Despair! The Brain
can scarce sustain the reflection, in our coolest
moments.'

Above the title, however, in pencil, are inscribed these words:

Any person who delights in good cock & bull
stories, here he will find them to his hearts content.

I remember the first occasion, as an inexperienced doctor,
that I was called upon to certify a patient dead. He looked
dead all right; and there is a certain *je ne sais quoi* about death.
But when, nervously, I put my stethoscope to his chest,
instead of hearing nothing at all, I heard all manner of
sounds. Was I imagining them? If not, what were they and
how were they caused? No one had told me what to expect.
The rumblings, gurglings and scrapings: were they the blood

running through my ears, the sound of the friction of my stethoscope on the skin of the corpse, or post-mortem changes taking place in his lungs?

I signed the form (the ward was busy), and as far as I know the man did not awake to new life in the mortuary. If truth be told, I was anxious not so much for him, as for myself and my reputation in the hospital. Imagine the mockery if I misdiagnosed death! Occasionally one reads in the newspapers of cases of the certifiably dead who have defied convention and come alive (and conscious) at the touch of the pathologist's saw. They are few – but then, post mortems, the final court of appeal of a doctor's diagnosis, are now very few also.

There was a whole literature on the subject of premature burial in the nineteenth century. Edgar Allan Poe was not alone. A late flowering of this literature, also in my collection, is *Premature Burial and How It May Be Prevented with Special Reference to Trance, Catalepsy, and other Forms of Suspended Animation*, by William Tebb and Col. Edward Perry Vollum MD, the latter late medical inspector of the US army, second edition 1905.

Vollum himself had a near-escape from premature interment (unless he was an unprincipled liar and made his story up). According to the preface:

> Dr Vollum first became interested in the important question of Premature Burial in consequence of his own very narrow escape from live sepulture, having been pronounced dead from drowning, and prepared for interment, when consciousness happily returned spontaneously.

Consciousness happily returned, but I doubt that it was a happy consciousness. Moreover:

> On more than one occasion Col. Vollum was instrumental in rescuing persons from the most horrible imaginable of fates, in spite of the opposition and ridicule of physicians, priests and relatives, who loudly protested against any delay in the obsequies of those whom they erroneously declared to be unmistakably dead.

The book contains descriptions (and illustrations) of various devices by means of which the dreadful eventuality might be avoided. There is, for example, the invention of Count Karnice-Karnicki, Chamberlain to the Czar of Russia and Doctor of Law of Louvain University. I cannot do better, by way of description, than to quote:

> Broadly speaking [the apparatus] consists of a long tube, about three and a half inches diameter, and a hermetically-sealed box. The tube is fixed into an aperture in the coffin as soon as the latter is lowered into the grave. No gases can escape from the tomb into the outer air, as the metallic box into which the upper end of the tube enters cannot be opened from the outside.
>
> On the chest of the supposed dead body is placed a glass ball, several inches in diameter, attached to a spring which communicates through the tube with an iron box above ground.
>
> On the slightest movement of the chest wall,

as in the act of marked breathing, or movement
of the body, the glass ball releases a spring which
causes the lid of the iron box to fly open immediately, thus admitting both air and light into the
coffin. At the same time a flag rises perpendicu-
larly about four feet above the ground, and a bell
is set ringing which continues for about half an
hour... The tube acts as a speaking tube, and the
voice of the inmate of the coffin, however fee-
ble, is intensified.

The apparatus, which is said to have cost about twelve
shillings, had been successfully tested on those who had vol-
unteered for mock-premature burial; and the authors hoped
to sell it throughout the United Kingdom.

Another method, adopted in the mortuary of Munich, a
truly palatial neo-classical establishment to judge by the picture of it, was to tie the extremities of the allegedly-dead by
means of a cord to a bell on their temporary biers. Off the
main halls of the mortuary was a caretaker's room, complete
with watering cans for the care of the elaborate plant arrange-
ments, and there (if the picture is to be believed) sat a lugubri-
ous-looking man in a uniform very like that of a railway tick-
et inspector of the era, waiting for a bell to sound. It is said
that a soldier's life is ninety-nine per cent boredom and one
per cent terror; this must have been even more true of the
mortuary attendant's job, though I suspect that the balance
must have been tilted – again to judge by his face, for in those
days people were entirely without electronic means of distraction – in the direction of the element of boredom.
(Recently in a large cemetery in Nottingham, I complement-

ed a gardener on the grounds; he thanked me, said it was a quiet job he did. 'The residents don't give us much trouble.')

It is difficult to know, of course, just how many burials, both in absolute numbers and proportionately, were – or are – premature. In a chapter devoted to this very question, we read:

> In 1829, arrangements were made at the ceme-
> tery, New York, as to bury the corpses in such
> manner as not to prevent them from communi-
> cating with the outside world, in case any should
> have awakened to life; and among twelve hun-
> dred persons buried six came to life again. In
> Holland... of a thousand cases investigated, five
> came to life before burial, or at the grave.

But the true moral of all this is that it is difficult to proportion our fears to the true dangers; for example, to be three
times as afraid of a heart attack supervening as a stroke,
because heart attacks are three times more common. And
thus, by the examination of one inscription and a little reflection on two volumes (the second 'nicely got up' according to
the contemporary criticism in *The Hospital*, and indeed it has
beautifully-gilded pages), we reach the largish and not unim-
portant conclusion that it is difficult for a man to be wholly
rational.

14

Scaling the Revolution

The premises of most second-hand bookshops are generally not select, because the volume of trade cannot sustain high rents, and so they are generally found in odd corners of cities or small country towns. Because of the problem of slow turnover and high rents, excellent shops are sometimes found where you least expect them. Once, for example, I had gone to a formerly-industrial town in the north of England to examine for the courts a man accused of murder. It was the kind of place of which there are now so many in Great Britain, and that was never beautiful to put it mildly, in which by far the largest industries were the public administration of unemployment and the attempted bureaucratic amelioration of social problems caused by cultural degeneration. 'Please help me,' the victim, who was lying drunk on his bed, had said to the murderer, a plea that the latter had interpreted as one for strangulation. In such a place, one might understand the error, though not of course forgive it.

Having time to kill – an expression that always brings guiltily to mind Richard II's prescient description of my life story, 'In my youth I wasted time, And now doth time waste me' – between the end of my examination of the murderer and my train, I found a second-hand bookshop of the most extraordinary excellence. In fact, I had asked a prison officer just before I left the prison whether he knew of such an establishment in the town, but he did not, and resorted to the yellow pages to help me. The fact that he did not, in a town not exactly filled with other attractions, brought home to me just how minoritarian my obsession with books really was.

As soon as I entered the shop, I regretted that I had so little time. I would happily have spent the day there. As I peered at the shelves, a man in late middle age approached me and asked whether he could help, and whether there was any subject that I was particularly interested in.

At that time I was in my Haitian stage. I had been to that country a couple of times, and its history had fascinated and moved me as no other (except that, perhaps, of Paraguay). Haiti had gone straight from slavery to disaster, long and continuous disaster, but its people were dignified, with little of the self-destructive hatred of their own lives of which I witnessed in a more developed nation.

'Haiti,' I said, expecting him to laugh.

'I think I might have a couple of things out at the back,' he said in that laconic Northern English way that I love, without evincing the slightest surprise (he was evidently used to people with strange interests and, like a doctor, did not express any disapproval of those who came to him with them).

And, within a few minutes, he had brought out not only Hazard's *Santo Domingo, with a Glance at Hayti*, of 1873, but much rarer and more precious, Charles Mackenzie's *Notes on Haiti Made during a Residence in that Republic*, of 1831, in such condition that it might have been printed and bound yesterday. This book is dedicated to James Cowles Prichard, MD FRS, who in 1835 used the words 'moral insanity' to delineate the kind of man – for it usually is a man – who is perfectly normal except in his moral faculties, and is therefore prone to behave in an antisocial way disagreeable or appalling to others: perhaps by mistaking a plea for help, for example, as one for strangulation.

One thing that can be said about booksellers is that they are not generally in the trade to make large sums of money quickly. This is not quite the same thing as being uninterested in money altogether, for there are still those among us (though far fewer than they once were) who believe that slow accretion over a long time is the best, surest and perhaps the most honest way to prosperity. Besides, one can be greedy in a small way as well as a large; a profit of a pound can excite cupidity in a small trader as much as can a profit of a million pounds excite cupidity in a big one.

I have never met a bookseller uninterested in his wares. Some are vastly more concerned with the adventitious aspects of books than with the meanings of the words they contain: for example, in the misprints to be found in one edition but not another (it is a curious thing that misprints usually add to the price, if not to the use value, of a book, just as a postage stamp printed upside down is always more valuable than its correctly-printed equivalent). But no bookseller I have ever known has treated books as if they were merely a means to his end, that is to say his own enrichment. For booksellers generally, the book retains something of the sacred quality that it had when it was written by hand.

One bookseller whom I knew much preferred his books to his customers, whom he regarded as a pack of philistines. Why he had a bookshop at all was a bit of a mystery; perhaps he valued the opportunity to annoy and humiliate people.

He seemed to have learned his method of dealing with the public from Soviet restaurants. His first defence against the public was to keep his plate-glass front door locked, though the notice said that it was open, and he and his staff (an old man employed part-time) could clearly be seen inside the shop. As an aside, never trust bookshops with a notice hanging on the door that says 'Popped out, back in fifteen minutes;' like Wagner, booksellers have their bad quarters of an hour.

The second defence employed by this bookseller against his customers was music: Schoenberg, to be precise. A short blast of Schoenberg is probably as effective as white noise in clearing any public space, and certainly it led in short order to the clearing of the shop. The customers, being more cultivated than a cross-section of the general public, would probably not have admitted that it was Schoenberg's music that drove them away – in fact they liked Schoenberg – but the sudden remembrance of an appointment.

His third defence against customers was to refuse to sell them the books that they had selected, on the grounds that they were not worthy of them. This happened to me once. It was at the time that I was writing a book about Liberia. I happened to find a history of Sierra Leone on his shelves, and of course the two countries have many things in common. I took it the counter behind which he was standing to pay for it.

'What do you want it for?' he asked.

Taken aback by his imperious tone, I answered weakly: 'I'm writing a book on Liberia,' I said.

'An academic book?'

'No. A travel book.'

'Then I don't think you need this.'

He slid the book under the counter, preserving it for a worthier purchaser, who could put the book to better use.

Instead of losing my temper, and calling him a bullying mediocrity who feared that others might be better than he, I simply snorted and walked out. But such was (and is) my avidity for books that I later swallowed my pride and, like a dog returning to its vomit, slunk back to the bookshop again, for sometimes the owner sold customers books in a relatively normal way and his stock was good. Bibliomanes are used to swallowing their pride.

I had had disagreements with him before when I had been writing my book about the civil wars in Central America. I took the view, unusual at the time I think, that these wars were not the expression of an immemorially downtrodden peasantry pushed beyond endurance, but rather the expression of the frustration of a class of young intellectuals at the scant importance accorded them in the current dispensation, an importance to which they believed themselves entitled by virtue of their intelligence and education.

That western intellectuals in their turn, particularly the young, projected on to Central America at the time all their own self-important revolutionary and utopian longings is more or less established by the scant attention given to these countries ever since their 'inevitable revolutions,' to quote the title of a book about the region by an eminent American academic, failed to take place. Once the countries of this region failed any longer to serve as plausible political paradises, and settled back into their traditional quotidian corruption, they might as well have sunk, like Atlantis, under the sea for all the interest that western intellectuals showed in them thenceforth.

The bookseller had a book about Nicaragua that I

wanted. It had been published about six months before and this copy had been read by someone with dirty thumbs and the habit of bending the pages. Nevertheless, I wanted to buy it, for it had information that I needed for my book and in those days, before the advent of the internet, it might not have been easy to find another copy, at least without the trouble of going to an exceptionally large bookshop.

I was mistaken in my expectation that the bookseller would sell it to me cheaply because of its rather disgusting condition. No, he wanted the full cover price for it because, he said, of the Net Book Agreement.

In those days, new books had a fixed price and retailers were not allowed to discount them. According to the bookseller, no book might legally be sold within twelve months of its publication at less than the fixed price, and therefore he was not at liberty to sell it to me for less.

'But you didn't buy it at the full price,' I said.

'That's different,' he said. 'I bought it by private treaty with an individual. I'm selling it publicly.'

'But its condition is terrible,' I said, changing the argument. 'I could buy a nice new pristine copy for the same price.'

'Well go and buy one if you want, or wait another six months when I'll lower the price. Its condition is irrelevant, and I'm not breaking the law.'

However unpleasant as a man I thought he was, I could not but help but admire his elevation of principle over economic self-interest. I returned him the book.

15

Discounted Souls

In France books may not be discounted by more than 5 per cent, an amount insufficient to motivate a person strongly to buy a book in one place rather than another. In Britain, a retailer may discount books at whatever rate he likes or thinks he can make a profit. This means that what costs £25 in an independent bookshop may sell for £15 in a chain. Even the most avid supporter of small local commerce might balk at paying 66 per cent more just to maintain it.

The results of the difference are striking. In Britain, the selling of new books (disregarding Amazon) is virtually a monopoly, at most a duopoly, a chain or chains of stores each of whose branches is virtually indistinguishable from the others except in size. In France there are many independent bookshops, no small town being without one, and each carrying a different stock. Except for the classics and the books of the moment, you cannot predict – unlike in England – what you will find in one bookshop by going into another.

Is this not a strange difference between, on the one hand, a country usually (but wrongly) deemed to be economically liberal and, on the other, one deemed to be economically statist? In one the market results in uniformity; in the other, state intervention (of a simple character) results in diversity.

What is to be said in favour of the English system? The first is that there are more than twice as many books published in Britain as in France, and therefore there is greater choice of reading matter in Britain. I doubt, however, that the legal right of booksellers to discount books is the reason for this. The English-speaking market is five times larger than the French-speaking one, and it is this that probably accounts for it.

Books – at any rate some of them – are cheaper in Britain than France. Practically no books are published in hardback in France, whereas most are in England, and often for more or less the same price. Whether this is an important difference is a matter of opinion an taste; I prefer hardbacks, but this difference in publishing practice also precedes by a long time the difference in selling practices, when both countries did not allow the discounting of books.

What interests me most, however, are the cultural effects, or at any rate manifestations, of the two systems. In England I live in a small and beautiful town that has a branch of WH Smith, its logo-shopfront defacing an early eighteenth-century building in true unabashed philistine fashion. In France I live near a small and beautiful town, somewhat smaller, that has two independent bookshops (one of them run by the mayor's wife). They are not offensive to the eye.

There is no doubt in my mind as to which is superior from the cultural point of view. WH Smith has a policy of concentrating on a few titles, ferociously discounted: on piling 'em high and selling 'em cheap. Such other stock as there is consists of past or would-be best-sellers at the trashy end of the literary spectrum, biographies or alleged autobiographies of celebrities, mainly from the worlds of sport, television and pop music, lurid books about criminals and the autobiographies of those who have 'survived' sexual abuse in childhood. There are no English, let alone foreign, classics. Even the mildest forms of scholarship are under effective ban.

By contrast, there is no such cheap trash in the French bookshops: I use the word cheap in its non-economic sense. True, the bookshops have a lot of crime fiction. But crime fiction is rarely trash; the standard of writing, to say nothing of the plotting, is often higher than that in supposedly more serious genres.

The intellectual level of the books sold is incomparably higher. I was not surprised, for example, to find there a biography of Proust's father, an eminent specialist in public health. (I hesitate to blow the trumpet of my own profession, medicine, but the fact is that not only were many doctors good or great writers, but the fathers of many good or great writers were doctors. Proust, Flaubert, Dostoyevsky spring immediately to mind.) I can go to the bookshops in the small French town – as in any other small French town – and buy not only the French classics, but many foreign ones translated into French.

The absence of emphasis on the sale of a small number of discounted titles generating huge and easy profits seems to result in a greater effective choice, and furthermore in a choice more worth making: that is, if it is accepted that worth is not wholly determined by crudely aggregated sales. The choice actually presented to the French public is better, greater and more intelligent than that presented to the British public; and while it might be argued that this superiority of choice is because the French public had better taste (and not only in books) in the first place, the causative relationship surely runs the other way as well. Taste is formed by what is presented to it; and under the British system what is presented to it, at least in very large part, is trash. The appetite grows with feeding.

Certainly, the two bookshops in France seem to contribute to a much higher cultural level evident in the streets in almost everything, from the faces of the people to level of municipal services. It is difficult to discern cause and effect in such complex matters, but who would dare to venture that the arrival of the store of a WH Smith-like chain would raise or even serve to maintain standards there?

The difference in the method of new book-selling in the two countries is not starkly that between a totally free market on the one hand and complete state control on the other. Both countries have markets in books, but differently regulated. Nor is the difference that between choice and absence of choice: 80,000 books a year are published in France, by many different publishers, and any book published in the whole world is available to the French public through the internet, just as it is to the British. But if you go into a French bookshop in the deepest provinces you do not get the impression, as you do if you repeat the experience in Britain, of a people with no connection to or interest in its own past, but only living with the television on.

Effective choice is not the same as choice. It is effective, not the hypothetical, choice that affect a people's *mores*.

Britain, because of the near-universality of its language, is a great centre, much greater than France, of scholarly publishing about every conceivable subject. But you would never know it from walking down any of its streets. Indeed, you would infer precisely the opposite. This raises the heretical thought – heretical, that is, for anyone suspected of an inclination to believe that the market as a solution to all human problems – that an indefinitely expanded range of products might not be all-important in the formation of the human soul.

16

Carting Harlots

One bookseller I know, whose shop is also his house, is a true bibliomane. His books keep accumulating in his house, so that the space left over for him to live in decreases all the time. He is not so much painting, as booking himself into a corner. He spends practically all the money he makes by selling books on buying new stock, and since, naturally enough, he sells dearer than he buys, the number of books keeps increasing. To put it in Malthusian terms, he sells arithmetically but buys geometrically.

The books have long since overwhelmed the shelves and are now piled, two or three deep and ten feet high, against the walls. Needless to say, this does not make it easy for the browser, who is inclined to suffer from an instance of Sod's law, namely that the book in which he is most interested should be very near the bottom of one of the piles. At another bookshop arranged on the same principles, I once had to be rescued by the bookseller from an avalanche of books when I pulled out a book (of plays by Sir Arthur Wing Pinero, now more or less forgotten but the most popular playwright of his day, and – as I discovered after my rescue – signed by him) from the bottom of such a pile. In the typical English manner, I apologised profusely to the bookshop owner, who replied complacently, 'Oh please don't mention it, it happens all the time.' There is still a small corner of commerce that is untouched by health and safety.

The Welsh were once great readers, though their taste (at least to judge from the second-hand bookshops, which are relatively plentiful there) is, or was, a little religious. But in the small town of Bethesda I underwent a conversion experience, the only one of my life. I found a small bookshop with a stock so tiny that the sale of all of it at once could hardly have been expected to keep the owner in heating and lighting for more than a month or two. I would have said that the woman who ran it did so more for social than for financial reasons: except that the passing trade must have been practically nil.

I found there a copy of a comparatively rare pre-war book on Cambodia. This, too, is an interest of mine. The mass murder in Cambodia has now reached its final stage, that of tourist attraction. Not only have the torture chambers of Phnom Pen become a museum, but hawkers walk around the temples of Ankor Wat selling tourists books about the Khmer Rouge era (so short in time, but so profound in effect that it is rightly called an era). These books explain all, after the fact of course, and I have been curious to discover whether, in any book written about Cambodia, before the Khmer Rouge, there was any inkling of what was to happen, any awareness that the country to which all the authors were so deeply attached – for no one ever wrote of Cambodia except with affection – was to become the scene of one of the most notorious mass killings in the century of mass killings. Needless to say, I have found none; we should all be wise before the event.

But there was another book in Bethesda that I bought: an odd volume of the works of the Lord Bishop of Bristol, the Reverend Thomas Newton, DD, printed in 1782. It was £5, and though in my life I have wasted thousands practically

without number, on such things as restaurants and cham-
pagne, and though I have unhesitatingly paid much more for
other books (I dare not tell, for fear it might be disclosed to
my wife, what I paid for *A Brief and Accurate Treatise Concerning
the Taking of the Fume of Tobacco, which very many, in these days, doe
too too licentiously use: In which the immoderate, irregular, and unsea-
sonable use thereof is reprehended, and the true nature and best manner
of using it, perspicuously demonstrated, by Tho. Venner, Doctor of
Physicke in Bath*), I dickered for several minutes over the Rev.
Thomas Newton and his £5.

At one time, I would never even have considered an odd
volume; I wanted the whole set, or nothing. Incompleteness
in set of works seemed to me a deep wound. This phase has
now passed, since there are very few multi-volume works that
I will ever read all the way through, from volume one to volume six or eight – besides which, complete sets are much
more expensive, often beyond my pocket, than odd volumes.

Moreover, and happily, I have found that the nectar can
often be sucked as well from a short reading of an obscure
work as from a long one. For example, not long ago I picked
up two of the three volumes of *The Ladies Library, Written by
a Lady, Published by Mr Steele' and 'Printed for Jacob Tonson, at
Shakespear's Head over against Catherine Street in the Strand* in 1714.
It was actually written by Joseph Addison, him whose style
Doctor Johnson praised so highly, and I found it in a bookshop in a provincial town from which, as far as I could tell, all
ladies had either long fled, been expelled, or in which they
stayed severely indoors, leaving the streets to bare-midriffed
women with voices that made the windows rattle. The preface
to *The Ladies Library* contains the following warning to readers:

> In Matters where both Sexes are equally con-
> cern'd the Words Man and Men are made use of,
> but the Matter does not for that Reason the less
> relate to Women, or argue that the Work is not
> primarily intended for the information of the
> Fair Sex.

Such usage would not be accepted today, as being beyond the
comprehension of literal-minded readers.

The volumes are full of admonitions to virtue, admonitions that so far at least have been unavailing: and generally, if
something has not succeeded in the first 300 years of its oper-
ation, it will never do so. Here is chastity:

> Of all the Christian Virtues, there is none that
> shews the Dignity and Power of the Soul so
> much as *Chastity*: 'tis a Triumph over the Desire
> which Nature has imprinted in the Heart of
> Man, fierce and unruly, full of false Hopes and
> imaginary Delights, which too often blinds the
> Understanding, and leads to Destruction.

But, as they say in Nigeria, you can't keep a goat from eating
yams.

The chance finding of the odd volume of the Lord
Bishop's works – a theological defence of the goodness of
God, a genre that one might be inclined to dismiss as the
oleaginously complacent musings of a man only too com-
fortably-placed in life, until one learns that the author wrote it
in response to the death in the same week of both his father

and his son – introduced me to a class of literature that, until then, I had spurned and even despised: namely, the writings of the seventeenth- and eighteenth-century English divines (excluding Donne).

Lacking religious belief, I assumed that those who had it must, as a consequence, have had nothing of worth to say to the world. A moment's reflection should have been sufficient to demonstrate to me that this was not likely to be true; they were just as intelligent as we, and much more cultivated; and they dealt with those subjects, such as morality and death, that remain not without resonance.

The trouble with not having had a formal literary education, especially in an age inclined to despise its forebears, is that one's knowledge is likely to have great lacunae. Nature hating a vacuum, a kind of positive ignorance, in the form of brute and brutish prejudice, rushes in where knowledge might have been. So it was with me and the divines.

I went straight from Thomas Newton, a lesser light, to perhaps the greatest of them all, Jeremy Taylor, and soon acquired a handsome copy of his *Holy Living and Holy Dying*, as well as a first edition (1647) of his plea for religious tolerance, *A Discourse on the Liberty of Prophesying, Showing the Unreasonableness of Prescribing to Other Men's Faith, and the Iniquity of Persecuting Differing Opinions*.

The irreligious have a tendency to assume something that is impervious to contrary evidence, namely that the religious are by nature persecutory bigots, held back from performing inquisitions only by lack of power to do so; and while Taylor's treatise is far from a plea for total toleration, for it assumes that all good men are Christians of one kind or another, it is far in advance in point of tolerance of much of the secular political practice of the twentieth century.

All I knew of Taylor before I read Newton was that Somerset Maugham (not exactly a religious fanatic himself) recommended him in *The Summing Up*, which for long I took as my bible of style, as having written some of the finest prose in the language. But on looking into Taylor (and other divines), I found it was not the style alone that was moving: it was their manner of thinking about human life from an eternal perspective. For example, the chapter *Remedies against Fear of Death, by way of Exercise*, in *Holy Dying*, for example, opens:

> He that would willingly be fearless of Death must learn to despise the world; he must neither love anything passionately, nor be proud of any circumstance of his life. O death, how bitter is the remembrance of thee to a man that liveth at rest in his possessions, to a man that hath nothing to vex him, and that hath prosperity in all things, yea unto him that is yet able to receive meat! But the parts of this exercise help each other. If a man be not incorporated in all his Passions to the things of this world, he will less fear to be divorced from them by a supervening death; and yet because he must part with them all in death, it is but reasonable he should not be passionate for so fugitive and transient interest. But if a man thinks well of himself for being a handsome person, or if he be stronger and wiser than his neighbours, he must remember that what he boasts of will decline into weakness and dishonour…

In other words, there is a kind of religious, or existential, equality as well as a political and economic kind, in the recollection of which a man may be encouraged to a laudable and justified humility not easily attained by any other way:

Dust thou art, and to dust thou shalt return.

The chance finding of a single volume of Thomas Newton, DD (at a cheap price), led me to consider more carefully the contents of the library of a close friend of mine. It had come with the house that he had bought from a family of landowners and churchmen, and half of which consisted of works of theology and collections of sermons, in eighteenth- and early-nineteenth-century editions. For more than twenty years I had not so much as taken one of those books down, not even from the idlest of curiosity; but now I began to read, and like numerous generations before me found some consolation in what I read, not only in the prose style, deeply resonant but at the same time supple, but also in the sentiment. Here, for example, is Joseph Hall, DD, Lord Bishop of Exeter and then Norwich, from which function he was destituted by Parliament in 1643, on the subject *Of the truly noble*:

> He stands not upon what he borrowed of his ancestors, but thinks he must work out his own honour; and if he cannot reach the virtue of them that gave him his outward glory by inheritance, he is more abashed of his impotency than transported with a great name.

And here, to the absolute tee, is the character of our former

Prime Minister, Tony Blair, in the character of *The busybody* as delineated by Hall:

> His estate is too narrow for his mind, and there-
> fore he is fain to make himself room in others'
> affairs; yet ever in pretence of love.

Hall was by all accounts a good man in practice as well as in theory, and I think his humanity is evident in his *Meditation on a Harlot Carted*, that is to say a prostitute taken away for pub-lic punishment:

> With what noise, and tumult, and zeal of solemn
> justice, is this sin punished! The streets are not
> more full of beholders, than clamours. Every
> one strives to express his detestation of the fact,
> by some token of revenge: one casts mire,
> another water, another rotten eggs, upon the
> miserable offender. Neither, indeed, is she wor-
> thy of less: but, in the mean time, no man looks
> home to himself. It is no uncharity to say, that
> too many insult in this just punishment, who
> have deserved more… Public sins have more
> shame; private may have more guilt. If the world
> cannot charge me of those, it is enough, that I
> can charge my soul of worse. Let others rejoice,
> in these public executions: let me pity the sins of
> others, and be humbled under the sense of my
> own.

It might be argued, of course, that the decent sentiment, however nobly expressed, is not enough to make men decent; and yet it would be rather odd if all the words in the world made no difference to anybody.

By strange coincidence, I came to live shortly after my fortuitous discovery of the English divines in a house next door but three to one that had briefly been the home of one of the most eminent of these divines, Richard Baxter, author (among many other works) of *A Saint or a Brute: the Certain Necessity and Excellency of Holiness*. It was a little whitewashed timber-framed sixteenth-century house on whose front wall were painted the following words:

> In this house lived the learned and eloquent
> Richard Baxter 1623 – 1626.

For some reason, I misread these words for more than a year. I read them as saying:

> In this house lived the learned and elegant
> Richard Baxter 1623 – 1626.

I was rather sad when I realised my mistake. I much preferred 'learned and elegant' to 'learned and eloquent.' The first sounded cavalier-ish, the second roundhead-ish. We do, after all, live in an age in which people find it difficult to distinguish between earnestness and seriousness.

17

The Fight Against Absurdity

One of the little collections within my library (though I have not pursued it with anything like the single-minded devotion of the true collector, merely expanding it as and when I happen to come across a book that will fit into it) is of books published during the years 1917 to 1940 in Britain, the United States and France about the Soviet Union. This collection establishes – as definitively as such a chance or unsystematic collection can establish anything – that all that Alexander Solzhenitsyn and Robert Conquest wrote in the 1960s and 70s and that finally persuaded the western intelligentsia that the Soviet Union was from the very first, indeed from the days immediately after the October Revolution, a monstrous experiment in mass killing, known and documented.

In effect, neither Solzhenitsyn nor Conquest revealed anything that was not easily knowable, if not known in the sense of being accepted as true. I have books with photographs of the massacre of priests, for example, in the immediate aftermath of the Revolution, and of the naked famine victims in the Ukraine in the early 30s being loaded on to carts and trucks for burial. It is not true that all that was written at the time was apologetics for the Soviet Union (the favourite titles in my collection being *The Soviet Union Fights Crime* and, even better, *The Soviet Union Fights Neurosis*).

In my collection is a book by George Popoff, called *The Tcheka: The Red Inquisition*, published in 1925. The German title was better: *The Tcheka: State within a State*. Popoff was also the author of *The City of Red Plague*, an account of the Soviet occupation of Riga in 1919. He is frequently described as 'anti-communist,' as if to be anti-communist were a kind of psychological quirk or spiritual sickness rather than the response of normal, decent and intelligent people to the horrors perpetrated by communists in their attempts to implement their doctrine.

I was pleased when I found the book, of course, but its inside cover was disfigured by a dreadful scoring-out of a previous owner's name with a black marker pen. In this instance, no name replaced it; the act was one of pure negation. A friend of mine suggested, when I mentioned the phenomenon, that it might be the old owner, ashamed at selling his book and anxious to destroy the evidence of his betrayal of it, and not the new purchaser, who performed the defacement, but I thought this unlikely: no one, not even the most neurotic, eliminates his own name with such venom.

By chance, I found another copy of the book, in pristine condition and very cheap, a little while later, but it was a second impression printed the following year. I had another friend who I knew would be interested in Popoff, so I bought it; but then I was confronted with a dilemma – with which of the copies should I present him? I wanted to keep the better copy for myself: but which was the better copy? Did the black scouring out neutralise the first copy's advantage in being the first impression? Did the cleanliness of the second copy neutralise its disadvantage in being a second impression? I am inclined to keep the second copy for myself, but have not quite decided once and for all, and so still have both copies.

The very triviality of this dilemma appals me, especially when I consider the world-historical importance of the subject-matter treated of in the book. Thirty million dead, and I am impaled on the horns of so tiny a dilemma. Could human insensibility go further?

Yet one does not eliminate a concern merely by pointing out its absurdity.

18

Darling Passions

Another example in my little library of the genre of expunging a previous owner's name with a black pen is on the inside cover of an unpleasant little book called *The Menacing Rise of Japan: Ninety Years of Crafty Statesmanship in Pictures*, published in 1943. On the cover is a caricature of a Fu Manchu-like figure; the foreword to the book is by the British diplomat, Robert Vansittart. However one may deplore political correctness as a deliberate attempt to limit thought, and however much one takes into account the horrors of what the Axis powers were doing in that very year of the book's publication, Vansittart's words now have a distinctly unpleasant ring:

> If ever two Allies were well matched, they are Germany and Japan. The German veneer is thicker, but beneath it the resemblances of pure savagery have always struck me as remarkable... here are two soul-mates, two twentieth-century nations with B.C. dispositions and mentalities. The Japanese seem, perhaps happily, to have achieved a record in the unlovable. There has been a little conventional patter about 'warlords,' but nothing like that pertinacious nonsense about only fighting Nazism and not the Germans. There has been no concerted

ostrichism in the case of the more natural – and
so less culpable – savages.

One of the curiosities of this book is that its co-author is Ernest Newman, the musicologist and critic whose learned and laudatory expositions of Wagner did more to popularise the most German of composers in England than any other single factor.

In the very year in which he published *The Menacing Rise of Japan*, he also published *Opera Nights*, suggesting that the combination of a profound emotional response to music and violent national hatreds was not entirely confined to the Nazis. As for Alexander Howard, the other author of the book, which is essentially a paean of hatred intended to inculcate that hatred in others, he too was capable of tender feelings, for it is inscribed by him as follows:

To you darling with all my love – as ever, Alex

On the inside cover is a narrow label, typewritten. 'THIS BOOK BELONGS TO:' – and then the name is eliminated with a heavy black pen, as is part of his (or her) address. The elimination is both careful and careless; it is careful in so far as it is confined to only certain elements of the label, but it is careless in the sense that it is without form, mere squiggles. This vandalism seems to me an act – a very small one it is true, but an expressive one – of brutality. Do people who mark books in this way behave worse than others? I like to think so, but have no evidence to prove it.

One unexpected example of the thick black pen eliminating a previous owner's name was to me unexpected and surprising: a new owner of the nine volumes of Father Copleston's *A History of Philosophy*, now in my possession (only temporarily of course), had gone through each volume and eliminated the name of the original owner with his black marker. Surely something more – well, more philosophical might have been expected of him than the desire to annihilate the name of the man who had the temerity to own these volumes before him (he didn't put his own name instead, perhaps fearing that it would suffer the same fate). The only difference between him and other annihilators of the names of previous owners of books was that, alone of all that I have come across, he did it very neatly and precisely, with as small an area of black ink as possible, helped by the fact that the previous owner was himself micrographic. Perhaps the annihilator was affected by the precision and minuteness of the distinctions made by scholastic philosophy, the very philosophy from whose standpoint Father Copleston wrote his great work.

The expunging of previous owners' names, though made easier and more thorough by the existence of marker pens, is no new phenomenon. In my second edition of Thomas Browne's *Pseudodoxia Epidemica: or, Enquiries into very many Received Tenents and Commonly Presumed Truths*, of 1650, a seventeenth-century owner's name is obliterated by ink that has turned brown.

This wonderful book commences with the memorable statement that 'The first and father cause of common Error, is the common infirmity of humane nature…' Dr Browne combats the misconceptions of his age. The urine of toads, for example, is not venomous because 'to speak properly, a Toad pisseth not.' Of the Jews he writes, 'That Jews stinck naturally, that is, that in their race and nation is an evil savour, is a received opinion we know not how to admit,' because the Jews 'must needs have suffered inseparable commixtures with nations of all sorts,' not least because 'their Women desire copulation... and affect Christian carnality above circumcised venery.' So the Jews being an impure race, more mongrel than any other, cannot have a biological property such as stinking: a very modern argument.

There was a great African collector of seventeenth-century books such as those of Sir Thomas Browne and Robert Burton, namely Dr Hastings Banda, the first president of Malawi. He bought them in the 1920s and 30s when studying in America, and they were comparatively cheap. A first edition of *The Anatomy of Melancholy*, such as Banda bought, would now fetch $50,000. It is surely remarkable that a man born to peasant parents in Nyasaland, as it then was, should have developed a passion for such books, when not one in a thousand of the people in the land in which they were written would give a fig for them; but Banda is said to have gone without food in order to buy them.

Not only was Banda a bibliomane, but he was a doctor, and therefore I felt a double affinity for him. But when I arrived at my hotel in Blantyre in 1976, I was handed a cyclostyled piece of paper, distributed I suppose to all newcomers. Some of its content burned itself into my memory, from which I now quote:

> The people of Malawi so love their Ngwazi [chief of chiefs] that if any visitor has come to Malawi in order to kill His Excellency the Life President Ngwazi [chief of chiefs] Dr H. Kamuzu Banda, the people will chop him up and

throw him to the crocodiles.

As tourist information, this struck me as distinctly odd. I wish only that I had kept that piece of paper, but in those days – still a young man, to whom the past was not yet more interesting than the future, and for whom the present would never develop into the past – I thought such ephemera worthless. Likewise, I did not buy one of the cotton-print cloths with a bust of His Excellency the Life President Ngwazi Dr H Kamuzu Banda printed in a roundel on it, that women wore as they ululated as his Excellency the Life President Ngwazi Dr H Kamuzu Banda went by, standing in the African heat in his open Rolls-Royce, wearing his dark three-piece suit and waving his fly-whisk.

Later I hired a car in Malawi, one of the conditions of hire big that if I happened across the motorcade of His Excellency the Life President Ngwazi Dr H Kamuzu Banda, I would drive the car to the edge of the road, get out of it, and stand to attention until the motorcade had passed. I suspect that His Excellency learnt his authoritarian ways as a general practitioner in Britain during the 1940s, and (as my patients used to say preparatory to uttering an evasion) 'part of me' admired him for it.

Be that as it may, the career of the Life President – who was, in fact, forced to stand down at the age of ninety-five – suggests that bibliomania is not incompatible with megalomania and other undesirable traits.

19

Comic Dictators

While on the subject of dictators, I should here relate one of the greatest of my regrets at the non-purchase of a book, a regret that has so far lasted nearly a quarter of a century. I was crossing Africa by public transport from Zanzibar to Timbuktu, and was in Libreville, capital of Gabon. The president at the time (as he was from 1967 until his death forty-two years later, whereupon his son took over) was El Hadj Omar Bongo, formerly – before his conversion to Islam for reasons not necessarily connected with religious truth – Albert-Bernard.

El Hadj was very short; he therefore banned the word *pygmée* from the French language, wore platform shoes and made sure that the press never photographed him looking shorter than anyone else in the photograph. The definition of a politician, I suppose, might be someone who believes that reality can be mocked.

The book that I did not buy was *Il était une fois El Hadj Omar Bongo*, a comic-strip biography of *le Grand Camarade*, as he was known at the time, which turned this notorious kleptocrat into some kind of nationalist hero. In the process it justified the one-party state as being more suited to Africa than any other, which was proved by the fact that he was subsequently elected by 99.6 per cent of the votes. The book was on sale everywhere in the city, and I knew that it would sooner or later become a period piece; however, travelling on public transport in rural Africa did not permit the accumulation of books, and I did not trust the post.

Later, I discovered that there was a French publishing company that specialised in such comic strip biographies of minor dictators, obviously paid for by themselves (that is, if one calls dictators' money their own). I procured two of them, the first in English about Siaka Stevens of Sierra Leone, and the second about Jean-Claude Duvalier of Haiti. The latter was said to be sponsored by the *Comité d'action Jean-Claudiste* rather than by Baby Doc himself, though this must have been the only time that Baby Doc's name was associated, even by implication, with the faintest semblance of a doctrine or a political principle.

What could *Jean-Claudisme* be? As it happens, the book did not reach Haiti straight away because the *Comité d'action* was not quite active enough to prevent his overthrow in whose aftermath the demand for Duvalierist literature was severely limited.

Eventually copies were imported for sale to visitors as curiosities, but unfortunately there were no visitors – except for me and my wife. I wanted to show her the country – called 'the best nightmare in the world' by Herbert Gold, who wrote a wonderful book of that title – with which I had fallen romantically in love.

We were eating one night in a restaurant where the only other customer introduced himself as the Minister of Tourism.

'Are you tourists?' he asked us.

'Yes,' we replied.

'You are not tourists,' he said, half-wearily, half-admiringly. 'You are heroes.'

I did, of course, buy a copy of *Il était une fois Jean-Claude Duvalier* from an itinerant salesman, and now the book, which makes the fat and not very bright son of his sinister father into a nationalist hero along the lines of El Hadj Omar Bongo, is not to be had for love or money.

I thought the Parisian company that published these comic-strip biographies of dictators would make an interesting article. Of all niche publishers, theirs was surely (if I may so put it) the nichest. There were many questions that I wanted to ask. Do dictators come to you, for example, or do you go to them? How large are the print runs, and how much the subventions? Who first had the idea of specialising in this unique genre?

Unfortunately they were not pleased to see me when I arrived. '*Nous avons changé notre activité,*' they said frostily, and with a finality that brooked no further curiosity on my part.

20

Positive Thinking

My copy of the revised and enlarged edition of Manson's *Tropical Diseases*, published in 1900, less than two years after the first edition, was owned and marked in blue and red by Dr Lyon Falkener, physician to the Western Fever Hospital, who died on July 5, 1952, aged 85, in a nursing home in Ealing.

Manson was a remarkable man and his book was a remarkable book. Having been appointed doctor to a lunatic asylum, he resigned and went to China instead, as doctor to the Chinese Imperial Customs. He then spent many years in private practice and research there, eventually founding the medical school in Hong Kong from which Dr Sun Yat-Sen, the first president of the Chinese Republic, was one of the first two to graduate. Manson went on to found the London School of Tropical Medicine and Hygiene (one of the great British institutions of higher learning constantly threatened with diminishment or closure).

More impressive still, it was Manson who discovered the insect transmission of disease, possibly one of the most important discoveries, from the point of view of public health, in the whole history of medicine. With almost infinite laboriousness, he established that mosquitoes transmitted the organism responsible for causing elephantiasis, the most dramatic pictures of which (for example, a scrotum necessitating a wheelbarrow) adorn, or adorned, all textbooks of tropical medicine of a certain era. And it was Manson who intuited, as a result of his discovery, that malaria might also be transmitted by mosquito, and it was he who guided Sir Ronald Ross in his work that established that it was indeed so.

Ross, incidentally, was a somewhat reluctant doctor, who would rather have been a poet, playwright, musician or (an odd alternative), a mathematician than a doctor. He was certainly polymathic. Generally, though, his verse has been derided, and it is true that much of it is unreadable; I have seen the poem he wrote on the day on which he finally established the mosquito transmission of malaria, whose anniversary he ever-afterwards celebrated as 'Mosquito Day,' described as doggerel, but it moves me:

> This day relenting God
>   Hath placed within my hand
> A wondrous thing; and God
>   Be praised. At His command,
>
> Seeking His secret deeds
>   With tears and toiling breath
> I find thy cunning seeds,
>   O million-murdering Death.
>
> I know this little thing
>   A myriad men will save.
> O Death, where is thy sting?
>   They victory, O Grave?

I quite see, of course, the various rationalist objections to the sentiments expressed in the poem, a piece of work that which

would no doubt infuriate the new breed of atheists. That Ross
sought the 'secret deeds' with tears and toiling breath is almost
literally true; often, in the years that he devoted to the task, he
despaired; the microscope he used is rusted with the sweat of
his brow; but is Death not here all but identified with God,
and if so how can God be good?

Why, one might ask, did He go to all the trouble to create,
or to permit, the malarial parasite to be a bringer of death to
millions (and much evil else besides), only to permit Ronald
Ross to discover its mode of transmission in 1897 after an
immensity of labour in Secunderabad? Besides, Death's victory is still complete; it is only postponed in some, or many,
cases, and certainly not turned into a final defeat. Of what
kind of divine plan would this be a working out?

One is reminded of the phrase in John Stuart Mill's
Autobiography, in which he records his father's objection to the
Christian conception that makes morality:

> … consist in doing the will of a being, on whom
> it lavishes indeed all the phrases of adulation,
> but whom in sober truth it depicts as eminently
> hateful.

Yet somehow this does not quite answer the case. There is a
depth of feeling in Ross' poem that is quite unmistakable. If
he had had an entirely naturalistic view of the world, he would
not have written it. The elimination of the providential view
of human existence tends to annihilate also any sense of gratitude for or wonderment at it, for what merely exists by natural process is soon enough taken for granted, as just being
there.

Naturalism destroys people's gratitude in the same way and for the same reasons that the continual granting of rights to tangible benefits destroys it; for when people receive those benefits they are no more than they believe themselves entitled to, and when they do not receive them, they feel a sense of injustice. Hence the modern personality oscillates between a disabused and pseudo-sophisticated ingratitude on the one hand and resentment on the other: neither of them very attractive as traits.

Ross was not the man of serenity that his poem might suggest, quite the reverse in fact. He was querulous and litigious, and after his great discovery spent a lot of time in a bitter dispute, over who had discovered exactly what, with the Italian parasitologist, Giovanni Grassi, who also claimed to have discovered the mosquito transmission of malaria. Ross was also tireless, and many would have said tiresome, in his attempts to secure monetary recognition for his discovery from the British government, repeatedly drawing attention to the £30,000 reward that parliament had voted Jenner for his discovery of cowpox vaccination. His failure stimulated him to write the following couplet, which might well serve as the motto of our increasingly clientelistic state:

> Who stands upright in Britain falls,
> He wins the prize of life who crawls.

Also among my books is one of poems by Ross, inscribed by him 'with respect' to another doctor, which contains verses he wrote when first sent out to India as a doctor in the Indian Army and found himself under-occupied and bored:

Here from my lonely watch tower of the East
   An ancient race outworn I see –
With dread, my own dear distant country, lest
   The same fate fall on thee.

O heaven, shall man rebelling never take
   From Fate, what she denies, his bliss?
Cannot the mind that made the engine make
   A nobler life than this?

But to return to Manson's book and its underlining: perhaps it is because I am a doctor, and therefore feel some retrospective solidarity with Dr Falkener, a previous owner and (as I have proof) its underliner. This is the one book in my possession in which it seems to me that words and phrases have been underlined throughout with the real intention of permanent assimilation into the reader's stock of knowledge.

When, opening it at random to page 544, the chapter on bilharzia, I see the words 'Recovery is rarely complete' neatly and finely underlined in the red ink that Dr Falkener employed, I feel sure that this is a fact that he guarded for the rest of his life. One can tell what did and did not interest Dr Falkener: for example, the chapters on cholera, dysentery and tropical sprue are all unmarked, while most of the others are most of the others are heavily but intelligibly marked. I have not been able to discover why some marks are in blue and some I red, but it is clear that Dr Falkener read with attention. In the chapter in yellow fever, written before the construction of the Panama Canal, Dr Manson wrote:

> With [the construction of such a canal] more
> direct and rapid communication there will rise a
> corresponding risk of spreading yellow fever
> into a large section of tropical humanity...

Dr Falkener has neatly scored out the word will with his fine
blue pen, and written the word 'may' in the margin.

The book gives rise to interesting reflections. Considering
how recently the mosquito transmission of malaria had been
discovered, it is astonishing how quickly and completely it had
been accepted, and how much of our present knowledge of
the subject had already been worked out by 1900. We pride
ourselves on the swift dissemination of knowledge, thanks to
the sophistication of our means of communication, but when
one considers how quickly cowpox vaccination spread, and
how quickly also the use of anaesthesia, one realises that we
are by no means so much in advance of our predecessors in
this matter as we sometimes like to suppose. Our vehicles go
fast, but our traffic jams slow us down.

In my youth I used to read philosophy, when Sir Karl
Popper's view of science, that no scientific hypothesis had
ever been proved but had only so far failed to be disproved,
was almost an unassailable orthodoxy. But is it really true that
we have only so far failed to disprove the mosquito transmission of malaria, or the circulation of the blood, and that
tomorrow we might wake up to headlines such as 'New
research proves mosquitoes do not transmit malaria,' or
'Blood found not to circulate in body but remains stagnant'?
Perhaps the accomplishments of medical science were not
worthy of Sir Karl's attention, as being only in the foothills of

the scientific mountain range, yet it is difficult to refuse altogether the name of indisputable fact to the mosquito transmission of malaria.

Another lesson from the book is the difficulty of wresting
truth from error. We too often and too easily take for
granted the progress that we have made – this means that,
just as many people are inclined to ask where poverty
rather than wealth comes from (as if wealth were the
natural condition of mankind), so many are inclined to ask
not where knowledge comes from, but ignorance. It is as if
they believed that a human being at birth knows everything
there is to be known, but that somehow in the process of
living he loses this knowledge and becomes ignorant.

Beriberi was a disease whose cause, when Manson
wrote his book, was still unknown. In fact it is a nutritional
deficiency disease, as was to be proved within a few years
of the publication of the book, caused by a lack of
thiamine (Vitamin B1) in the diet, and so especially
common when the diet consists only of milled white rice;
it is characterised by a disorder of the peripheral nerves
and also of the heart. But, because it frequently appears
epidemic, and for other reasons, Manson thought that it
must be a 'germ disease.'

Manson, after all, lived through the heroic age of
bacteriology, when not only bacteria but other organisms
were proved to be the cause of diseases. He himself had
contributed mightily to the advance in knowledge of these
diseases. What more natural, then, than that he should

think that a disease that 'is a place disease like malaria,' and is 'fostered by damp, by high temperature, and by its most often attacking those who sleep on or near the ground,' and in which overcrowding 'has a good deal to do with its frequency and virulence in such conglomerations of humanity as are found in Oriental jails, schools, mining camps, plantations lines, armies, ships,' should be caused by bacteria. Manson thought that the causative germ, whatever it was, did not act in the same way as other pathogenic germs, rejecting the claims of two bacteriologists, Pekelharing and Winkler, to have found it.

> My view of the matter [he wrote] is that beriberi is a germ disease; that the germ resides in the soil or in the houses and surroundings of beriberi spots; that it there distils a poison which, on being absorbed by man, produces neuritis...

This accounts for why no germ had yet been found in sufferers, why people who were removed from 'beriberi spots' to hospital often recovered, and why they relapsed when returned to their native environment. 'This is the only hypothesis,' he continued, 'which fits with all the facts of the case,' an hypothesis, he goes on to say, is supported by the following evidence, provided by a Japanese researcher:

> Of fifty-two infants who suffered from beriberi while being wet-nursed by beriberic mothers forty-two recovered, five died, five

were not accounted for. In the cases which recovered [this statement underlined in red by Dr Falkener] the improvement set in at once on the children being weaned.

Dr Falkener was not an uncritical reader of Manson, for in the margins against the statement 'True rheumatism is rare in the tropics,' and against several other statements, he has written a question mark. But on the infective nature of what he calls Beri Beri, he largely or in outline agrees with Manson. I know this from a slip of paper, marked L. F. [Lyon Falkener] 1 Sept. 02 that I found in the beriberi chapter. It is written in blue ink, but with some red underlining.

1 that the cause is a <u>germ</u>.

2 it may be the <u>diplobacillus</u> mentioned by Capt. Ross IMS [Indian Medical Service] (*Lancet* 9 Aug 1902)

3 this germ thrives in mouldy and damp <u>rice</u>: hence the frequency with which rice has seemed to be a causative agent – but it also probably thrives in <u>other media</u> where warmth and damp coexist.

4 people with open wounds seem specially liable to infection, hence the germ or its virus may enter by <u>inoculation</u> – it may require <u>repeated dosing by inoculation</u> to prolong its effects – hence the rapid recoveries on removal to a non infected site –

5 to explain the fact of its importation to new but suitable locations it is not necessary to hold

that the germ <u>thrives in the human organism</u>, it would do equally well if it <u>thrived in foodstuffs or other imported material</u>.

6 its love of warmth and damp render <u>over-crowding in warm and damp compartments</u> exceedingly dangerous.

I find this all moving and, in an odd way, inspiring. Here are highly intelligent and honest men, trying to take into account all the evidence at their disposal, groping their way towards the truth, but in the end failing to find it.

It required a leap of the imagination to see that it was not the presence of something, but its absence, that caused the problem. Even the Dutch doctor, Christiaan Eijkman, who won the Nobel Prize for showing that chickens fed white rice developed an illness akin to beriberi went to his grave believing that it was a positive poison in the white rice, not the absence of a vitamin, that caused the problem.

What Manson and Falkener show, however, is that it is possible for people to think about something in an honest and disinterested way, which is something that has long and vehemently been denied by various schools of thought.

21

Bohemians & Foreigners

I may be thought a dangerous person when I mention that I have a little collection of books with graphic representations of suicide by hanging. I can claim a professional interest in this, since I have had more than an average amount to do in my career with people who have tried this means of ending their life having in my time examined between 10 and 15,000 people who have attempted suicide. I was once even involved in a case of murder by hanging, the murderer having given his victim the choice between being hanged or strangled to death. The man chose to be hanged, which the perpetrator then tried to pass off as a suicide; I forwarded quite a lot of evidence to the contrary to the police, and the man was duly convicted. I have resuscitated hanged men – one of whom, by way of thanks, attempted to sue me afterwards – and also certified them dead.

But none of this explains my collection, more attributable to prurience than to scholarship, though prurience of a limited extent, since the collection has formed adventitiously rather than by deliberation. I have not sought out the books in it, but bought them when they came my way.

The two *pièces de résistance* of the collection are *Le Pendu de Saint Pholien*, The Hanged Man of St Pholien, by Georges Simenon (1931) and *The Anatomy of Suicide* by Forbes Winslow (1840).

The Simenon is one of the first Inspector Maigret novels, a cheap paperback when first published, but cheap no longer. Its paper, deeply yellowed and rendered brittle by age, has a distinctive smell, for English and French books smell different. The cover has a slightly lurid black and white picture, by an artist called Lecram, of a man hanging from the gargoyle of a church tower, which intrigues immediately because it is not easy to see how, even with assistance, he could have got there.

In the novel, he didn't get there. The hanged man of the title hanged himself at the easily-accessible entrance to the church, not from a gargoyle on the tower. But the reader is not disappointed because the tale is so satisfyingly atmospheric. Simenon, who was of course Belgian, often returned to the Liège of his early life, or the region of the Meuse, as the setting of his books. It is curious how often great writers have taken superficially unpromising provincial life (no one's heart leaps at the sight of the Meuse) for their subject matter: does subject matter make great writers, then, or do great writers make subject matter? By the same token, the most magnificent scenery seldom evokes the greatest landscape painting: why not?

Simenon *was* great. He had the gift of simplicity without simplification, and – whatever his unattractive qualities as a man in real life – he displayed as a writer real feeling for the frailties, the passions, the hopes and self-deceptions of ordinary men and women. By his pen he makes the ordinary, the quotidian, interesting; and the banal landscape of the Meuse becomes romantic without romanticism. The reader sees the world anew, and one can hardly ask more of a writer than that.

Le Pendu has a plot whose denouement the reader cannot

guess, but insistently wants to know. Simenon does not plant clues along the way whose significance the alert readers of whodunits may pride themselves in having spotted, and the unalert kick themselves for having missed. But the story is not the whole point of the book, or its only interest; central to it, perhaps surprisingly for a man of Simeon's unconventionality, is a good satire on artistic bohemianism.

The main characters are a group of men who, ten years before the action, formed as students an association called the Companions of the Apocalypse – in Liège. They thought they were all artistic geniuses, destined for the career of Rembrandt, but in the event their careers turned out ordinary, with varying degrees of financial success and happy family life.

During their student days, however, they discussed philosophy late into the night, as students do (or did, when there were fewer of them), in an atmosphere of wine, smoke, semi-darkness, unpaid rent and poverty. This is the atmosphere in which absurd and extreme notions, inflamed by 'a melange of Nietzsche, Marx, Moses, Confucius and Jesus Christ,' can seem urgent and compelling. One of their number, Klein, raises the question of whether it is easy to kill, from the psychological point of view, and sets out to demonstrate that it is. The victim is one of the Companions of the Apocalypse, a relative outsider, a Jew called Willy Mortier, the only one of them in easy circumstances, and therefore the object of their secret envy. Klein kills him and the group dumps the body in the Meuse, where it is never found, and no investigation ever mounted. Klein is then so filled with remorse that he hangs himself at the entrance of the church of St Pholien. The group disperses, pursuing life elsewhere, in Paris, Bremen and

Rheims. Another of their number, called Lecocq d'Arneville, is increasingly haunted by this suicide – he too is remorseful, and believes that the other members of the group, who have tried to forget the past, should be made to pay. He blackmails them, not to enjoy the money (which he burns), but to make their lives suitably wretched. And thus the baleful consequences of the bohemianism of youth are terrible and long-lasting.

I came to anti-bohemianism by a different route, having been by nature inclined to and attracted to the bohemian life. In the first place, I noticed that bohemianism derived its meaning from being the opposite of, or at least by teasing, respectability. Where there is no respectability, there can be no bohemianism; it loses its point, its sting. So great were the social changes wrought in the era of my young adulthood that respectability became the new Bohemianism: convention, be thou my revolt.

There was something more, however. In Africa, and elsewhere, I came to see that truly poor people, those who could not assume that there would be enough to eat on the morrow, wanted desperately to be clean, tidy and neat. When they achieved it despite all the obstacles, their cleanliness, tidiness and neatness represented a triumph of the human spirit. Those people in rich countries who lived in avoidable squalor and went around scruffily, with artfully torn jeans, were not so much expressing their solidarity with the poor and wretched of the earth, as they fondly imagined that they were doing, but distinguishing themselves from them. Ever afterwards, I felt a visceral dislike of the fashion for dressing down, for looking poor when one was nothing of the kind. It was as if there had been a mass outbreak of Marie-Antoinettism, with everyone playing shepherdess without so much as clapping eyes on a sheep.

Forbes Winslow's book, by contrast with Simenon's, has a remarkable frontispiece. Forbes Winslow was a psychiatrist, or alienist, whose son, of the same name, and also a psychiatrist, was perhaps more famous than he, principally for having made suggestions as to the solution of the Jack the Ripper case. As far as I know, no one has yet proposed Forbes Winslow as the Ripper, though almost everyone else of consequence at the time has been so proposed.

The Anatomy of Suicide is generally said to be the first medical text in English devoted to suicide, though I think this is a mistake. It is usually referred to rather slightingly, as being intellectually confused and without lasting value. The author is unable to make up his mind whether suicide is a crime, or the result of an illness to be compassionated. Certainly his intellectual performance is grossly inferior to that, say, of the sociologist, Emile Durkheim, fifty years later. Forbes Winslow attempts to classify neither the acts of suicide nor their causes; his very few statistics are rudimentary. But the book is not without interest or charm.

In the first place, some of the clinical stories told by Winslow are recognisable today: for example, of a suicidal woman who believed that she had killed her child and would not be dissuaded from her delusion even by being brought, alive and well, the very child whom she claimed to have killed by strangulation. She simply said that the child, though it resembled hers, was another; she persisted in believing that she had wickedly done away with her child. I had a case exactly similar a hundred and seventy years later.

Winslow is actually quite acute on the fleeting kind of suicidal ideation that can afflict even the normal (assuming, that I, whom am my own standard of comparison, am normal). He describes a man who thought of suicide because of the sheer tedium of drawing on his clothes every day. Winslow also describes the momentary suicidal impulse that many people feel when exposed to a great height:

> There are hundreds who cannot approach the brink of a cliff, or ascend a lofty tower, without experiencing an almost invincible desire to precipitate themselves to the bottom…

'Almost invincible' is an exaggeration, for if the impulse were really such it would be yielded to much more often than it is; but certainly whenever I have visited the great waterfalls – Niagara, Iguazu, or Victoria – I have approached with the thought that it would be easy and perhaps advisable to put an end to all my petty miseries, present and to come, by throwing myself down them.

I have approached the edge nearer the edge than officially permitted, in order to let chance take over. Then I remember the study of people who had thrown themselves with suicidal intent from high buildings, but survived. More than half of them regretted what they had done as they were falling, perhaps the most genuine and intense example of regret known to man.

The frontispiece to the book is of a bizarre variant of human suspension. A young man with a crown of thorns who has nailed all his limbs to a cross save for his right arm hangs from a window in Naples suspended in a net. He did not die and did not repeat the attempt, but according to Winslow remained of melancholy mind for the rest of his life.

Forbes Winslow vibrates with outraged national pride at the suggestion that the English, because of their foggy climate, are particularly prone to suicide, a charge levelled at them by, amongst others, Montesquieu.

> The charge is almost too ridiculous to merit serious refutation. It has clearly been established that where there is one suicide in London, there are five in Paris. In the year 1810, the number of suicides in London amounted to 188; the population of Paris being near 400,000 less than that of London. From the year 1827 to 1830, no less than 6900 suicides occurred; that is, an average of nearly 1800 per annum.

The French commit suicide so frequently because they are a frivolous, irreligious and light-minded people:

> The causes which frequently lead to self-destruction in France are, defective religious education, *ennui*, and loss at dice or cards.

He goes on to cite an instance:

> 'Will you dine with me today?' said a Frenchman to a friend.
> 'With the greatest pleasure; – yet, now I think of

it, I am particularly engaged to shoot myself; one cannot get off *such* an engagement.'

'This,' comments Winslow, 'is not suicide *à la mode* with us.' On the contrary, we are a serious people:

When we do shoot ourselves, it is done with true English gravity. It is no joke with us.

This reminded me of a passage in the memoirs of one of the last hangmen of England, Albert J. Pierrepoint. He was once asked whether people struggled on their way to the scaffold. Pierrepoint replied that he had only ever known one to do so; 'and he,' said Pierrepoint byway of explanation, 'was a foreigner.'

This in turn reminds me of Arthur Koestler's remark about the English and hanging in his book written against capital punishment, *Reflections on Hanging*. It was written at a time when this age-old ritual was under severe attack, and Koestler, who knew what it was to be condemned to death, having spent several weeks under such a sentence in a Spanish gaol during the Civil War, wanted to add his mite. The English, he said, do not seem to mind being hanged; 'in fact,' he added, 'they seem quite to like it.'

Yet even his attitude was not completely unequivocal, for in his *Spanish Testament* he admitted that he felt more free and happier while awaiting execution that at any other time in his life. 'Depend upon it, sir,' said Dr Johnson, 'it concentrates a man's mind wonderfully when he knows he is to be hanged in a fortnight;' but concentration of mind is not quite the same as the feeling of freedom and happiness.

How could Koestler have felt freer and happier under sentence of death than at any other time in his life? I suspect that it was because he was liberated from all the extraneous business of life, the constant anxieties and vexations, that in his condemned cell he was in as pure a state of being, without distraction, as it is possible for a human being to achieve. He was in a condition the very opposite of that of the man described in Addison's *Spectator* who hanged himself to avoid the intolerable annoyance of having to tie his garters every day, and for whom, according to Madame de Stael, the flight of time was marked only by the swift repetition of petty troubles.

One could, of course, make a collection of those authors who had been condemned to death and reprieved: Dostoyevsky, Koestler and Herman Charles Bosman, for example, the latter the greatest writer whom South Africa has produced (he shot his brother-in-law dead during a quarrel). Whether being condemned to death is good for writers and literature is an epidemiological question of some methodological complexity, however; I do not venture an opinion.

22

Dirty Words

Another interesting question is whether censorship is good for literature. Personally, I rather suspect that it is. Certainly most of the greatest literature in the world was produced under conditions of censorship; and freedom to say anything does not seem to have raised the average standard much, let alone resulted in hitherto unscaled peaks of beauty and significance.

Of course, censorship can crush the life out of literature when it is very heavy, but so, in a different way, can liberty. Writers are an undisciplined lot on the whole, and a little bit of benign and capricious censorship is like hanging, it concentrates their minds wonderfully. Would Turgenev have been so good had he not had to approach matters obliquely? What operates on the mind indirectly has the most effect. I am with Emily Dickinson:

> Tell all the Truth but tell it slant –
> Success in Circuit lies
> Too bright for our infirm Delight
> The Truth's superb surprise
>
> As Lightning to the Children eased
> With explanation kind
> The Truth must dazzle gradually

Or every man be blind –

A little light censorship, mild and incompetent, favours the implicit, while freedom favours the explicit. Moreover, once explicitness is let loose, it tends to become a savage god, demanding more and more sacrifices to itself. What once seemed daring soon becomes tame or trite, and is forgotten because surpassed; invention becomes synonymous with the desire and necessity to gain momentary attention by extremity of expression. The whole business is self-defeating and becomes a bore; and a sophisticated person is one who draws the line at nothing.

I have a small collection of illicit books, or rather, books that were once illicit. My copy of *Lady Chatterley's Lover*, for example, claims to have been printed in Florence in 1929, by the Tipografi Giuntina directed by L. Franceschini (the liberality of Mussolini's regime being so well-known). In fact, it was printed and published clandestinely in London in 1930 by the Anarchist bookseller (!) Charles Lahr and the Australian writer, and later supporter of the Axis, P.R. Stephenson. In the attempted suppression of *Lady Chatterley* we see the baleful effect of censorship: it made a bad book seem attractive and important.

Perhaps it was because Lawrence was himself so ill at the time that he wrote it that he did not see how shockingly callous, how completely lacking in common humanity, it was to make of the paraplegic Sir Clifford a symbol of the sexual repression of the age. Not a single word or expression is wasted on sympathy with the suffering of a man who has been shot in the spine during the war and paralysed from the waist downwards. Some of the writing is absurdly bad; only a man with no sense of humour could read of the twinkling of Lady Chatterley's buttocks without laughing.

After the prosecutor Mervyn Griffith-Jones asked, in his opening address, whether it was the kind of book you would want your wife or servants to read, and the jury all-too-understandably tittered, there was no possibility of a conviction. It is a cruel fate for a man of integrity, as was Griffith-Jones, of whom no evil is known, to be remembered in history only for a single fatuous remark made in court. Though it must be asked whether the coarsening of culture that Griffith-Jones predicted in his address would result from the wide dissemination of the book was any less realistic than the fulsome praise lavished upon it by critics who were called as witnesses for the defence, many of whom, I suspect, perjured themselves grossly in their evidence, so eager were they in the cause that they were supporting, and said things that they did not for a moment believe.

My prize illicit books come from the same era. They are volumes wrapped in old newspaper and were brought to my mother by her bohemian cousin who lived in Paris in raffish literary circles. In those days, when respectability still existed, bohemianism had a point and was viewed by many as subversive and dangerous. Moreover, it was still possible to live in the centre of capital cities on practically next to nothing if one was prepared to forego the comfortable amenities of life. Bohemianism is now nothing but a struggle against an open door.

My father, no paragon of respectability himself, nevertheless detested my mother's cousin, more I suspect from personal antagonism towards her artistic and intellectual pretensions than from any apprehension of real danger. A very beautiful woman, she dressed in dark, polo-necked sweaters and wore a lot of mascara. These accoutrements turned her, according to my father, into some kind of Jezebel, though he himself was a womaniser from whose attentions no female in his office was ever safe. I even have a half-brother, of whom I know nothing except his existence. Such, however, are the contradictions of moralists, or should I say moralisers.

My mother's cousin lived in the Latin Quarter and wrote poems, published in ephemeral magazines of impossibly low circulation. Of her poetry I remember only one line, from a love poem:

As mine as you are not...

It stuck in my memory for some reason at the age of ten when I first read it, and actually it seems to capture quite well the hopeless longing, the almost physical ache in the heart, that is unrequited love, from which I was subsequently to suffer more than once.

My cousin was a mistress for a time of the black American expatriate writer, Richard Wright, author of *Native Son*. Once when I went to see my cousin in Paris, where she continued to spend three months of the year after having moved to Australia. We went to Père Lachaise where Wright's ashes rest, to put flowers by them. My cousin told me about his death from an alleged heart attack shortly after he had been treated in the American Hospital in Paris for chronic amoebic dysentery, and she believed he had been assassinated by the CIA. Wright, after all, had been a communist, and was very publicly opposed to many aspects of American policy and society. I said that I thought that there was an alternative explanation of his death. The treatment of amoebic dysentery at the time was with emetine hydrochloride, which was known to be potentially toxic to the heart.

Somewhat to my surprise – I think aspects of naivety will remain with me till I die – my cousin was not pleased with this information; I realised that she *wanted* Wright to have been murdered, which would, I suppose, have given her the *frisson* of having been peripherally associated with an important cultural event, the assassination of a significant writer.

When she arrived in England for her brief visits from the Latin Quarter, she brought my mother books covered in brown paper or in newspaper – works that were banned in Britain at the time. (Prohibition of books in Britain was because of sex, in France because of politics.) I should have thought that wrapping books in news or brown paper would have made the life of any customs officer very easy; it was a virtual admission of obscenity, in fact, as then defined.

The books were the memoirs of Frank Harris and the novels of Henry Miller, published by the Obelisk Press, an English-language publisher founded by the Manchester-born writer, Jack Kahane, that veered between high modernist seriousness, or earnestness, on the one hand, and outright pornography on the other.

Another of the newspaper-covered volumes was *The Limerick: 1700 Examples, with Notes Variants and Index*, published in 1953 under the imprint *Les Hautes Etudes*, which as far as I know printed nothing else. The author was a man called Gershon Legman who had two great interests, *risqué* folklore including jokes and poems, and origami, the Japanese art of paper-folding. It is said that he was the first man to make of dirty jokes a serious academic study. Certainly, his collection of limericks, with etymological notes and geographical variants, is testimony to his diligence and erudition. But try as I might to celebrate the infinite variety of human learning, and to keep in mind that all phenomena are worthy of scholarly attention, at least by one or two people in the world, I cannot quite keep from my mind the thought that a lifetime spent in the study of naughty rhymes (and the like) has not been entirely *well*-spent.

I find the newspaper covering of the book rather more interesting than its contents. When one opens the book at random, the limericks themselves often appear so tame, lame and innocent of lewdness, that it seems odd that precautionary measures to evade customs should ever have been necessary:

> There was a young girl of East Anglia
> Whose loins were a tangle of ganglia.
> Her mind was a webbing
> Of Freud and Kraft-Ebing
> And all sorts of other new-fanglia.

What percentage of the population, I wonder, would understand the allusions to ganglia and Kraft-Ebing? I almost feel like going down into the street and conducting a survey to find the proportion of the population to which the name Kraft-Ebing meant anything at all. In England, I should imagine, Kraft-Ebing would be taken mainly as a poetic way of describing the decline of embroidery.

The cover of the book is a tattered and yellowing page

from the *Guardian* for November 30, 1959, mainly about the Labour Party Conference of that year. Aneurin Bevan, for example, thundered that the Tories were quite unable to challenge countries like Russia and China because modern capitalism had failed,' and that there would be a challenge to Britain not from America or France, but from Russia and China where, he said, people were beginning to reap the material fruits of public planning and ownership' (such as, for example, the famine caused by the Great Leap Forward, then at its apogee, which was the worst famine, as measured by numbers of victims, in the whole of history). There were appeals for tolerance in the party, which had suffered a wave of expulsions for Trotskyism:

> Dissatisfaction with the way in which members had been dismissed from the Labour party because of 'disruptive activities' was expressed by speakers on Saturday.

The reverse side of the page is somewhat less political. An article, 'The pop that makes Christmas go with a BANG!' is that of the wine bottle as the cork is extracted:

> Wine is as much a part of a proper Christmas as the pudding! Perfect for parties… the crowning touch to a wonderful Christmas dinner… wine brings its own glowing friendliness to the friendliest season of all.

The article goes on to tell the reader not to worry if he is inexpert in his choice of wine because 'your merchant' will 'glad-

ly suggest' what is right for you. And below is a further suggestion to readers that 'Old English glasses are among the
most charming objects to collect,' being 'easily obtainable and
costing from a few shillings upwards.'

Great Leaps Forward and expulsions of Trotskyists, then,
on one page, a middle class gentility very soon to die, in the
very process of dying on its reverse. It is not only religion that
had its long, melancholy withdrawing roar, but respectability
too. The gathering middle-class revolt against respectability is
evident in the following item:

> In most towns there is a need for a centralised,
> responsible and – yes – respectable baby-sitting
> service.

The need for respectability in a baby-sitting service is clearly
an embarrassment, and is therefore apologised for.

'Respectable' has become a dirty word, almost
unmentionable in polite society; it is oddly appropriate, then,
that this page should have been used to wrap a book
prohibited (but not for much longer) because of its
lewdness. But, all the same, a respectable service 'was
recently established in London by a bright business-like
young man of 33,' 'married to an actress and with a child of
4' – 'so he knows the difficulty.' The bright business-like
young man of 33 would now be an octagenarian, if he
survives, and the child in its sixties. When I think of this, I
am invaded by a bittersweet melancholy, that is, or at any rate
results in, an almost physical sensation around my heart.

The world of fifty years ago is as irrecoverable as that of
400 BC. Truly one cannot step into the same river twice (or

perhaps even once, as Cratylus said). One reads the following paragraph:

> It would be interesting to work out exactly how much time the working housewife – not to mention the wife who combines home and career – wastes 'holding-on' to a telephone whose caller seems always to be called elsewhere at the exact moment when communication is established. A day of it frays the nerves unendurably.

The solution to this grave problem is a device called the Fonadek, which 'is a sort of loudspeaker cradle on to which the receiver is placed,' so that 'the voice at the other end is magnified to a pitch that can be heard well across the room,' leaving the waiting person free to do something else that waste time.

I have mentioned Jack Kahane, the publisher of the Obelisk Press. He died in Paris shortly after the outbreak of the war, which perhaps was just as well for, as a foreign Jew, he would probably have been deported and killed during the Occupation in any case, as would his son, Maurice. But the latter changed his name to that of his mother, Gerodias, who was not Jewish, and he survived to carry on his father's work after the war. The Obelisk Press became the Olympia Press, whose ninety-four titles were smuggled into England until 1964, when permissiveness rendered illicitness obsolete. All the Olympia Press's titles were published in identical, instantly recognisable but sober olive-green covers, a kind of manufacturer's guarantee of salacity within.

My favourite among them is the last but one title to be published, *Murder vs. Murder: The British Legal System and the A6 Murder Case*, by Jean Justice. It is an examination of the case of James Hanratty, the last but seventh man to be hanged in Britain; it is an extremely strange book, at once reticent and self-revelatory.

Jean Justice was the son of a Belgian diplomat. He grew interested in the trial of Hanratty, accused of hi-jacking a car, killing the man who drove it and raping his lover, when his own homosexual lover, a barrister, gave him an entry to the much publicised trial. Like many another, Justice became convinced of Hanratty's innocence. In addition to that, he was also convinced of the guilt of a man called Peter Louis Alphon.

In order to prove this, he befriended Alphon and had a torrid homosexual affair with him, that clearly went well beyond any attempts to entrap him into a confession of his guilt. (Alphon *did* confess, but his word was as reliable as that of an average British contemporary cabinet minister.) If it is possible for something to be explicit while remaining between the lines, this book was explicit about the affair, which is presumably what necessitated its publication in France rather than England. A
mong other curious things, Alphon once tried to strangle Justice, but Justice nevertheless continued to see him. This is by no means implausible, since many of my female patients had been attacked many times in this way by their lovers, boyfriends, consorts or *partners*.

'Does he strangle you?' I would ask them, when I suspected as much.

'Yes, but not *all* the time, doctor,' they would reply.

Of course, when he (the strangler) was nice, he was very nice – just like Alphon, according to Justice.

As partial evidence of Hanratty's innocence, Justice publishes some of the letters that Hanratty wrote while awaiting execution. Hanratty was illiterate, and so wrote them by dictation to prison officers, and it would be a hard heart, I think, that would not be touched by them. In his last letter to his brother, on the eve of his execution by hanging, he wrote:

> Well, Mick I am going to do my best to face the morning with courage and strength and I am sure God will give me the courage to do so. Mick now you are the eldest in the family and I know that I could not count on anybody better than yourself. Mick we always got on well together and we had many good times together over the years. But I am going to ask you to do me a small favour, that is I would like you to try and clear my name of this crime. Someone somewhere is responsible for this crime and one day they will venture again and then the truth will come out. Time is drawing near, it is almost daylight, so please look after Mum and Dad for me.

Evidence suggests that Hanratty was, in fact, guilty, but even so the words, 'Time is drawing near, it is almost daylight' are terrible in their simplicity when you know what daylight means for him. I know of no words simpler or more powerful, unless they be Gloucester's reply to the old man when the latter tells him that he cannot see (Gloucester's eyes have been put out):

> I have no way, and therefore want no eyes.

Of course, the ability to say something moving or eloquent is evidence neither of goodness or innocence. The murderer, Jack Henry Abbott, wrote letters of literary merit to Mailer, who then used them to campaign for his release. Six weeks after it was obtained, Abbott killed again. As Abbott wrote, 'Books are dangerous where there is injustice.' But the injustice can be in a man's heart, from which books will not necessarily eradicate it, and indeed can inflame it further.

23

Stealing Time

Recently I entered a second-hand bookshop that was new to
me. It managed somehow to combine dustiness and
dampness. Shabby, ill-lit and disorganised, with a grumpy
woman unwillingly holding the fort for the absent owner at
an overcrowded desk, it was the kind of establishment
which sets the heart of the book-lover racing with
excitement, as brilliantly-lit and animated department stores
can never do. Never mind the silver-fish and other insects
mummified in the yellowing pages of old books that give off
an acrid smell when you open them, that catches you in the
back of the throat and makes you almost gag. Perhaps there
is an unrecognised treasure on the shelves that is patiently
awaiting its liberation to a more congenial and appreciative
home, that is to say your own library.

Squeezing myself into the narrow spaces between piles
of books on the floor and the stacks, I pulled out a volume,
now eighty years old, that I thought might interest me. It was
one of those that book-sellers are inclined, both in their
catalogues and inscribed micrographically in pencil on the
inside cover, to call scarce. Never, for obvious reasons, do
they point out that those who might actually want to buy the
volume are scarcer still.

The book itself I soon discovered to be of no interest to
me; but the hand-written inscription on the inside front

cover quickly and indelibly inscribed itself on my mind:

This book is stolen from…

When I look at the thousands of volumes on my shelves, the accumulation of a lifetime, an indivisible unity, I put their inevitable fate out of my mind, and imagine that nothing can part us. Even when I pick up a volume in my possession, three hundred years old, and see inscribed in it the names of its successive owners, I do not conclude that I am but its temporary guardian, and that my guardianship is merely a brief episode in its long history. No, I conclude that, at long last, the book has found its *true, rightful and final* owner, that I am the goal, the denouement, at which the previous three hundred years has been aiming. How easy it is to uncover the delusions of others, even when one shares them. Once, working as a doctor, I had two men on the same ward who claimed to be, and were convinced that they were, Haile Selassie. With what peals of derisive laughter they greeted the claims of the other.

In my more lucid moments, I know what will happen to my books. My widow, who will find them an encumbrance, will call in some dealer or other, who will offer her *yardage*, that is to say a certain small sum per bookshelf-yard. True enough, many of the books in that yard will be worth a few pounds at most, but one or two (the bookseller doing his best to disguise the shine in his eyes) will be worth hundreds or even thousands. The bookseller will present himself as doing my relict a favour, sucking air through his teeth, and claiming that the transport alone will cost him more than the books are worth. Finally, much against his better judgement, he will agree to take them off her hands, and she will be forever grateful to him.

Booksellers are, in fact, as dependent on death as much as undertakers for their livelihood. Once a friend of mine, an eminent scholar, died, and a dealer offered his legatee a derisory sum for his books. True it was a small collection, but it was select, with (for example) early editions of Adam Smith. I persuaded his legatee, who in her grief would have accepted the first offer, to demand much more, which the bookseller, thwarted, agreed to pay.

It is not always grief that aids the bookseller, but rather greed. One of the fraternity in Wales – I will not be more specific – once told me that he is sometimes called to a house with the corpse still on its deathbed, to buy there and then the antiquarian books that the house contains. The relict or other legatees present fear that absent legatees would make difficulties over the division of the spoils, and they would rather have the whole of a small sum than a fraction of a larger one. Whether this is economically sound from the point of view of the relict and legatees who are present in the house is beside the point: it is the denial of the inheritance to others that is so vitally important to the human heart.

I prefer to avert my thoughts from the posthumous break-up of my library. To me it seems to possess an obvious organic unity, that of my whole life, but I cannot expect an outside observer to notice it. A close friend of mine, on looking over my books, once said that, in the case of most personal libraries, he was able to tell at once what the owner's interests had been, his profession and probably his character too; certainly, I remember once reading that Professor Ullendorf's personal library about Ethiopia contained 6,000 books, so that no great powers of detection were needed to guess what his area of academic interest was. But with me, said my friend, my library offered no clue. Several special sections on Russia, Haiti, Albania, Liberia, Guatemala and Romania, along with criminal trials, poisonings, Doctor Johnson, anti-vaccination literature, bubonic plague, the Baconian theory of Shakespearean authorship, opium and Joseph Conrad, among other subjects, which were not large enough to be those of a real scholar, but were too large to be those of the mere general reader, gave no clear clue as to the nature of my interests, character or mental life.

Perhaps so. In optimistic moments I tell myself that I have found the world so interesting that I have been unable to confine my attention to any one subject; in pessimistic ones, that I am by nature lazy and impatient to have done so, with the result that my mind is like a magpie's nest, full of bright things, perhaps, but overall a mess.

Nevertheless, the prospect of the destruction of my library grieves me much more than that of my own death. This will no doubt strike all but book-lovers as profoundly strange, but I am far from the first to feel like this. The famous (or infamous) bibliophile of Barcelona, a former monk turned book-dealer, Don Vincente, who went so far as to kill people to take possession of their rarest books which he then kept for himself, said at his trial that he did not mind what happened to him, so long as his library remained intact. There were other peculiarities in the answers he gave at his trial that indicate just how far bibliomania may go in distorting a man's sense of proportion. Asked why, when he killed his last victim, a rival bookseller called Augustín Paxtot, he did not steal the money that was lying about, he replied indignantly, 'What do you take me for, a thief?' And when asked whether he had any remorse for having killed Paxtot, he said that he did. He killed his rival for a book that he believed to be unique in the world, but he had since discovered that there was another copy in a Parisian library. This fact derived his act of its higher purpose.

I do not kill for books, nor have I ever stolen one, at least if stealing be to take with the intention permanently to deprive. Of upwards of 10,000 volumes in my library, only three are borrowed but not returned, though not returned more because I have lost touch with their original owners than because I am so attached to them that I cannot bear to part with them (they are banal, and of no particular value). I have lost far more books to loan myself, and so my conscience is comparatively, though perhaps not entirely, clear.

The conscience of book-lovers is often somewhat elastic: the thieving bibliophile Tallemant des Reaux said that stealing books was not really theft, provided that one did not sell them afterwards. The man who stole rare books on Diderot's behalf, though not on his orders, said that the books he took would have been stolen if he had taken them for his own purposes, or if at least they had been useful to their owner. But it was at least four years since the owner had even entered his library, and therefore he expected that the books would be more useful, more productive of knowledge, in Diderot's hands. What more sensible and just, he asked? And, indeed, this is the kind of utilitarian thinking that guides almost all modern thought about social questions today.

24

An Overdose of Growing Up

The question of why the contemptuous treatment of books should so upset people is of some interest. After all, books are but physical artefacts, often mass produced and very rarely the unique copy in existence.

So great a literary figure as Doctor Johnson had no respect for books as physical objects; he is described as reading tigerishly, as if he would tear the content from the pages and the pages from their binding, bending the covers back so that he could bring the pages nearer to his all but unseeing eye (the portrait by Sir Joshua Reynolds of Doctor Johnson reading bears this description out). If a book exists in many copies and many editions, and moreover has been reduced to digital form available to all on the internet, what does it matter if a copy of the original edition, albeit centuries old, is destroyed? Indeed, those who themselves possess such a copy might rejoice at the destruction, in so far as it will tend to raise the price yet further.

A good friend of mine has never understood the mania for first or rare editions; after all, *Jane Eyre* is *Jane Eyre* whatever the edition (assuming that it has been faithfully reprinted). The argument that bibliophiles have been collecting first and rare editions almost since the invention of printing cuts no ice with him: it is merely another example for him of the immemorial folly of mankind.

The arguments, indeed, are all on the other, or his, side. The original edition may be badly printed, in need of correction; it may be fragile and therefore difficult to read; it may be incomplete and revised editions be much expanded and improved. If the purpose of books is to be food for thought, then the nourishment should be the best possible.

And yet the charm of first or rare editions, even when they are not beautiful in themselves, remains undiminished for those who feel it, and the prices demanded suggest that they are still not a few. Of course, this may change with the decline in the habit of reading of books, brought about by the availability of the written word in other forms. Newspapers, it seems, are about to disappear; why not books also, now that they are not necessary? This is a melancholy thought for me, who has spent all but a lifetime acting on the belief that books are almost as important as life itself, and much more reliable. I am like a craftsman who has spent a lifetime mastering a difficult skill, only to see it rendered completely redundant by the invention of a machine that performs ten times better and a hundred times faster than the best craftsman.

Yet I am not really pessimistic, at not least for long, when I recall Gibbon's explanation of the rapid triumph of Christianity over the established religions of the ancient world. Gibbon says that:

> … that it was owing to the convincing evidence
> of the doctrine itself…

Nevertheless, continues Gibbon, factors other than evidence were involved:

> As truth and reason seldom find so favourable a
> reception in the world, and as the wisdom of
> Providence frequently condescends to use the
> passions of the human heart, and the general cir-
> cumstances of mankind, as instruments to exe-
> cute its purpose, we may still be permitted,
> though with becoming submission, to ask, not
> indeed what were the first, but what were the
> secondary causes of the rapid growth of the
> Christian church?

Applying this insight to the question of the attraction of first
and rare editions, then, I comfort myself that what Gibbon
calls 'the passions of the human heart' – those irrational
promptings which we seek in vain to eliminate – will probably
sustain the markets for at least the remainder of my lifetime,
notwithstanding the rationalist assaults of my friend. Truth
and reason not finding a favourable reception in the world,
readers will continue to delight in the variations in old title and
half-title pages, however absurd they know in their hearts their
delight to be. The march of folly is a long one.

There is, of course, not only the question of first and rare
editions, but of inscribed, signed and association copies. The
modern marketing ploy of authors, who sign piles of their
books in bookshops while people queue at the table behind
which he sits, reduces somewhat the allure of modern signed
copies, which are now virtually mass-produced. Indeed, it
sometimes seems that authors have signed so many of their
books that unsigned copies are bibliographically the rarer (as
are their second editions than their first). No doubt for dif-

ferent reasons, many, perhaps a half, of the nineteenth-century medical treatises in my possession are inscribed with the
author's spidery compliments to a named, or a named but
illegible, or an unnamed recipient: the demand for such treatises being confined largely to such as were known to their
authors.

What is it about such signed or inscribed copies that pleas-
es? I again know what my rationalist friend would say. How
can the signature of the author add to the value of the contents, the only real value a book has? In most cases, you can't
even be sure that the alleged signature or inscription is really
that of the author.

For example, my copy of *On Asthma: Its Pathology and
Treatment*, by J.B. Berkart MD, published in 1878, is inscribed
'*To Thomas Nunn Esqu from the Author.*' Dr Berkart is entirely
forgotten, notwithstanding that his book is highly intelligent,
learned and stands on the cusp of new scientific understanding of disease processes; and, being now forgotten, even in
the recent history of asthma by Professor Jackson, it is almost
impossible that I should be able to verify that the writing is
actually his, at least not without an immense expense of
labour for a result of extremely doubtful value. But even if
the signature were proved to be his (and it is difficult to see
why anyone should go to the trouble of forging it), my friend
would still ask what more do I gain by its presence in the book
than by reading an unsigned copy? Once again, it would not
easy to answer convincingly.

This is all the more true of association copies, that is to say
(for those not acquainted with the term) those copies that
once belonged to a prominent person, and upon which he or
she left a distinguishing mark. (There has been an inflation in

the number of such copies, for an interesting reason: the
internet as a tool for more or less idle research.) Many years
ago, for example, before the internet could turn anyone into
an expert on any subject within five minutes, I bought a first
edition (for no more than a paperback edition would have
cost) of John Ruskin's *Unto this Last*, his four famous essays
lamenting and decrying the disenchantment of the world by
mass production and industrialisation. Inscribed in it, in the
flowing hand that masters of the old-fashioned nib pen so
skilfully managed, but with which I, in my childhood, when
such pens were still used as a pedagogic tool, could produce
only an inky mess, was the name *Robt Longsdon*. Years later I
looked Robert Longsdon up and found that he, or at any rate
a man of that name, was the business partner of Sir Samuel
Bessemer, inventor of the industrial process by which steel
could be produced in mass quantities. Surely it would have
been too much of a coincidence that a man with the same
name as that of one of the founders of industrial society
should have bought a book about the evils of that society, and
yet not be that founder himself? Therefore, I concluded, my
Robert Longsdon was *the* Robert Longsdon, the partner of
the man whose process caused me considerable misery in my
youth, as I struggled to reproduce diagrams of it for the purpose of examinations.

So what, asks my sceptical friend? Have you gone on to
inform yourself more deeply about Robert Longsdon, his
career and influence? What mental benefit, therefore, have I
derived from the book with his signature that I would not
have derived from a paperback copy without a single addi-
tional mark?

Authors and those well-known enough that their signature

on a book renders it an association copy rarely write anything very revealing that casts a light upon their lives or upon their character. This, too, my rationalist friend would use in favour of the absurdity of the desire of the bookman for such copies. The presence of a mere name or, at best, a brief and usually formal inscription, adds nothing to the possessor's knowledge or mental equipment.

Occasionally, of course, inscriptions do tell us something interesting. For example, in my copy of *How Britain Rules Africa*, by George Padmore, published in 1936, is a revealing inscription. Padmore was a West Indian communist, pan-Africanist and campaigner against colonialism. On the inside front cover is pasted a flyer for a public meeting or demonstration against the sending of British troops to Palestine by the Pan-African Federation in Trafalgar Square, to take place on what was to become my birthday thirteen years later (some people find these coincidence of extraordinary interest and significance, though a world insufficiently complex for coincidences inevitably to occur is almost unimaginable). The meeting was to be chaired by Padmore, and one of the speakers was to be S.C. Mukerjee, an Indian communist. It was to the latter that Padmore inscribed the book:

> To the leader of the Black Batallions – Mukerjee.
> For unity against the common enemy – British Imperialism.
> For victory over the White Scoundrels.
> With the author's compliments,
> George Padmore
> London 12.8.36

This inscription demonstrates the importance of race in the perception of injustice. Would Padmore have written in the same vein to Mukerjee if the races that oppressed their homelands had been different, say Arab and Chinese respectively? Post-colonial injustices at least as great as colonial ones have not called forth the same depth of feeling because they were committed by people of the same ethnicity as those upon whom they were practised. A little inscription thus opens a window on to a chamber of the human psyche that we would rather keep closed.

When I look a the writing of an author in a book, I become for an instant an amateur graphologist, though I think the science is probably bogus, and divine the character of the person from the character of his script. For example, I have a copy of a first edition of *Journey without Maps* by Graham Greene to a man called Anthony Hobson (whom I have not been able to trace, who does not appear in Norman Sherry's 2251-page long biography of Greene, and who, I suspect, might have been one of those people who approaches an author for his signature). Greene's writing is both angular and spidery, and almost micrographic, not that – I surmise – of a straightforward man with nothing to hide and an addiction to truth.

This divination of character is not quite sound, however, from the scientific point of view. Having read many of Greene's books at one time or another, and also something about him, I did not come to the inscription completely unprejudiced.

Even the book itself, an account of a journey on foot through Liberia, contains passages that caused me to suspect layers of insincerity and self-dramatisation to Greene's character. For instance, he describes how he discovered a will to live, previously absent in him, during a fever from which his companion on the journey, his cousin Barbara Greene, who also wrote an account of it, thought he was going to die. Greene writes, in a section titled *A Touch of Fever* (which he sought to cure by heroic doses of Epsom salts dissolved in tea):

> I had discovered in myself a passionate interest in living. I had always assumed before, as a matter of course, that death was preferable.
>
> It seemed that night an important discovery... I should know that conversions don't last, or if they last at all it is only as a little sediment at the bottom of the brain. Perhaps the sediment has value, the memory of a conversion may have some force in an emergency; one may be able to strengthen oneself with the intellectual idea that once in Zigi's Town [where he had the fever] one had been completely convinced in the beauty and desirability of the mere act of living.

I find this passage (which its sudden change to the impersonal 'one') about as convincing as the letter left to her parents by an adolescent who took an overdose, saying, 'Dear Mum and Dad, I'm sorry, I guess I've got a lot of growing up to do.'

25

Arsenic and Raspberries

One of the delights of a large library or a bookshop, especially a second-hand one, is that there is simply no knowing in advance what to expect. To let your mind roam freely, with no object other than to make unexpected connections as a result of that roaming, is one of the best ways of losing yourself in sheer disinterested delight: and the ability to lose yourself is a much more important ability in life than that of being able to find yourself, with its inherently immodest supposition that what will be found will be good and fascinating.

Second-hand booksellers tell me (and so it must be true) that young people nowadays do not like to browse among books. Of course, the phrase 'young people nowadays' should alert us to the possibility that we are merely lamenting the passing of our own youth in castigating those who are still youthful; old men have been doing so for centuries and millennia. But while we should be aware that unconsummated warnings of forthcoming disaster have been the entertainment of ages, we should also be aware that forewarned disasters do sometimes happen.

This is what the booksellers, whose declining numbers is, at first glance, evidence of their credibility in the matter, tell me: that young people, if they come into their bookshops at all, ask them whether they have a copy of x, usually something that they have been assigned to read by their teachers, and if they do not, that is the end of the matter. It does not occur to them to look round; it would seem to them a waste of time. They cannot know, then, the pleasures of serendipity, for their view of books is entirely an instrumental one, a means to an end, say the completion of an assignment. They have been brought up in an educational environment in which everything that is taught is of supposed relevance to their lives as they now are, or soon will be; indeed, any lack of such relevance is an alleged explanation of their ill-behaviour or refractoriness in learning. The notion that the *irrelevance* of subject matter to their current lives might enrich those lives and enlarge their outlook, by increasing what counts as relevant for them, is utterly alien. We live in an age that praises diversity and imposes uniformity.

Naturally, it will be suggested that *browsing the internet* is a higher, and more effective, form of browsing than that in bookshops. For a start, the internet is practically infinite in the information it contains, whereas a bookshop is severely limited by its stock. And then, at a mere press of a finger, a connection can be made. In bookshops, there are physical obstacles to be overcome; everyone knows that the books on the top shelf, that require a ladder to be reached, are likely to remain undisturbed for longer than those at eye level, whatever their relative merits.

I have put the argument to booksellers who splutter with rage in reply. Browsing on the internet, they say, is not at all the same thing as browsing among unknown books; it does not establish the totally unexpected and random connections that are, often at any rate, at the origin of genuine creativity. True, if you follow the links on a website, you will soon be far from your original subject matter, just as a child's question, *Why?*, leads after four or five steps to the most fundamental question of all, why is there something rather than nothing? But the links are ready-made for the internet browser, and it is their very rationality, their obviousness if you will, that renders them less valuable. The mind of the internet browser is passive by comparison with that of the book-browser, and he therefore cannot experience the *Aha!* moment of the latter that is like an intellectual orgasm.

I do not know whether this is true, or whether it is what a bookseller would say. As there are few young book-browsers, so there are few young second-hand booksellers. Perhaps the higher end of the market, which I have never been able to afford to inhabit, will survive, for very rare and very beautiful books might remain trophy objects for the very rich, as are paintings, say, by van Gogh. But the lower and intermediate levels of the trade, at least as carried out in shops, are almost certainly dying out. The dealers who remain at those levels increasingly trade from home by means of the internet, without the overheads and other inconveniences of shops.

The internet is both the saviour and the destroyer of the trade. It is the Shiva of bookselling. One internet site, for example, claims to have posted on it more than 100,000,000 books. It is undoubtedly a wonder, a friend of the researcher who needs a particular volume and no other. In the old days – when were they, was it five, ten or fifteen years ago? The pace of change is so rapid that one has difficulty in remembering one's condition of life even a twentieth of a lifetime ago – he would have had to rely on chance to find it, and might have sought it unsuccessfully for years, or upon a book-finder, a person who knew all the bookshops and which were most likely to have a copy. This profession is now as redundant, though it was perhaps never quite as much fun, as that of witch-finder, for it ended in a consummation less gratifying to the lurking sadism of mankind. Could, in fact, books go the way of witches?

One can 'browse' the 100,000,000 books all right on the abovementioned website. One enters a word or a phrase that embodies one's interest, and, after a delay of fully two seconds, an astonishing array of books comes up, more than one ever knew were devoted to the subject. At another touch of the keys one can arrange them alphabetically by author, by highest or lowest price, by reported reliability of bookseller, and so forth. One is humbled, almost crushed.

Some time ago I conceived an idea to write a history of arsenic in the nineteenth century. I thought that the subject was one whose ramifications raised interesting and important questions of social history. But it was obvious that to write the book required a great deal of information and study; it was not the kind of book that one could write from reflection on the experiences of a lifetime. I began to accumulate a large number of books of relevance to arsenic in the nineteenth century (and I even had an extract of the green cover of a book of the era analysed chemically in the toxicological laboratory of the hospital in which I worked, suspecting – correctly – that it owed its green colour to an arsenic dye).

Thanks to the internet, the accumulation of an arsenical library was easy. I found an American publication of the 1870s that consisted of pages of wallpapers that contained a lot of arsenic. I was surprised to discover that it was not just papers dyed with Scheele's green that did so, but many pink, blue and yellow papers as well. The nineteenth century was definitely the arsenical age (the land around the old mines of the English

Arsenic Company in Cornwall is still denuded of vegetation, more than a century later).

My collection – preparatory to the still unwritten book – was limited only by the depth, or rather the shallows, of my pocket. I could not afford to buy rare Portuguese treatises of the early nineteenth century on the medicinal use of arsenical compounds, for $5000 or more. In a way I regretted this, for once the collector's mania takes hold of one, one wants a complete collection, that is to say (in this case) every book, every document ever published relating to arsenic, at least in languages that one can read. But at the same time, even if I had had enough money to attempt seriously to do so, it was a curiously unsatisfying way of collecting. It would be like buying a ready-made collection, there would be nothing of me in it. If I went into a bookshop and found a section marked 'Arsenic in the Nineteenth Century,' next, say, to 'Women's Writing,' I would be mortified, though I would buy the lot if I could. Moreover, it is just a fact of human psychology, or the psychology of some humans, that it is one thing for a man to lay out $20,000,000 of his vast fortune for a Rembrandt, and quite another to find a Rembrandt for sale for $10 in a junk shop. The latter, I need hardly say, is (or perhaps I should say would be, given the unlikelihood of either) infinitely more satisfying to me.

I suppose it is a little like the attenuated pleasure that raspberries give me, now that they are to be had the year round. In my childhood I looked forward with intense longing to the raspberry season that lasted just a few weeks at most.

I still like raspberries a lot, so much so that I rarely resist them when I see them, which is frequently. I understand the miracle of human organisation, perhaps assisted by genetic engineering, that is involved in bringing soft fruit in a matter of hours from the raspberry-fields of Chile to my table many thousands of miles away within a matter of hours. But yet the intensity of the pleasure, the ecstasy, is not there. To adapt slightly he words of Henry V:

> If all he year were eating raspberries,
> To feast would be as tedious as to fast;
> But when they seldom come, they wish'd for come...

Yet I do not think there would be the same childhood ecstasy, either, if I were to deny myself all year round, and consume only raspberries grown locally during the season. The fact that they were available, and the fact that I had self-consciously decided to limit myself in order to restore the ecstasy, would be enough by themselves to destroy the ecstasy by making it artificial.

It is not just the fulfilment of his desires that he wants, but he wants them to be fulfilled in just the right way and no other. This, of course, could easily result in an infinite regress of desiderata.

Be that as it may, I have explained why a book about arsenic found in a bookshop specialising in books about railway trains will give me infinitely more pleasure than finding a much rarer and more valuable volume on the internet, even at a bargain price.

Alas, I have left my arsenic book too long: someone has written it instead of me. Professor James C. Whorton has written *The Arsenic Century*, and it pains me to have to say that it is excellent.

26

Heaven and Hell

It is strange how unpleasantness sticks in the mind so much more vividly than the opposite, which is why, I suppose, that it is so much easier for a writer to create a memorable villain than a memorable hero. Goodness, alas, is less interesting than evil, perhaps because it is less various, as Heaven is less interesting than Hell. Once, when I went to an island in the South Seas, I entered a church erected by missionaries who had instilled a sense of sin into what used to be called the natives. To the left of the altar (as the congregation sat) was a mural of Hell; on the right of Heaven. The former was very animated; little black devils with red eyes were boiling the naked damned in everlasting cauldrons, and poking them with their tridents to see whether they were done yet (they never would be, of course). Heaven, by contrast, was rather dull; a man in a Panama hat was walking along the esplanade of what looked uncommonly like an English seaside town on a Sunday afternoon, *circa* 1952.

Why is it that Man can so easily imagine Hell but not Heaven? If you asked me to imagine Hell, I could provide a hundred plausible Hells in ten minutes; but Heaven I could not begin to describe. *Eating pâté de foie gras to the sound of trumpets*, said the Reverend Sydney Smith; but you'd soon feel sick, to say nothing of the tinnitus.

I later heard a rumour that one of the book-sellers mentioned earlier abused (by which I mean beat) his elderly assistant, who certainly gave the impression of being frightened of him. I don't know whether the rumour was true – it probably wasn't – and yet my wish that it wasn't true was not without equivocation. The old man was perfectly pleasant, certainly much nicer than his boss, and I did not wish him an harm or unhappiness. And yet the thought occurred to me – and would not go away – that, while any individual evil was to be abhorred and reprehended, yet we needed it in order to know what good was, as Durkheim said we needed crime and criminals so that social solidarity might be expressed by the non-criminal majority.

Nevertheless, I stopped patronising the bookshop in case the rumour was true. My bibliomania, I am glad to say, has – at least so far – its limits.

27

Scalp Hunting

There was a time when I would not buy a marked book. A marked book was to me what unpasteurised cheese is to Americans: impure and contaminated. About twenty years ago, however, about the time when still lifes became my favourite genre of painting (having up till then rather despised them), and chamber music began for me to imbue much orchestral music, especially of the nineteenth century, with a quality of rodomontade, I began to see not the merits, but the great interest, of markings in books. I have now reached the stage when I will even buy a book for its markings rather than for itself. Only the other day, for example, I bought in Dublin a copy of Johann Georg Zimmermann's *Solitude Considered, with respect to its Influence upon the Mind and the Heart*, printed in 1824, purely for the inscription (in fact, I have another, earlier copy, under the rather more resonant title of *Solitude; or, the effects of occasional retirement on: The mind, the heart, general society, in exile, in old age, and on the bed of death. In which the question is considered, whether it is easier to live virtuously in Society or in Solitude. To which are added, the life of the author, notes historical and explanatory by the translator.*

Zimmermann was a doctor, a man famous in his time, who wrote not only on solitude but on bacillary dysentery. A Swiss, he was appointed physician to George III, but only in Hanover; Catherine the Great wanted him to come to

Petersburg, but he refused, probably wisely, to go. He was doctor to Frederick the Great during his last illness, wrote a memoir of his royal master which is generally regarded as having been both inaccurate and self-serving, and then went mad, dying in 1795. I think it fair to say that he is not much remembered now, but his *Solitude* is full of interesting insights. He says, for example, that there are solitary men 'to whom even the visits of friendship are displeasing,' and 'who, to avoid painful intercourse, confine themselves eternally at home, and consume their hours in writing books or killing flies.' I am not quite sure whether these alternatives are meant to be categorical or dimensional: whether those who do not write books kill flies, and *vice versa*, or whether those who write books decline by degrees into killers of flies, in which case it would be interesting to know what the intermediate stages, in both directions, are. At any rate, I remain for now at the book-writing end of the spectrum, though perhaps age will shift me flywards.

The inscription in the book, dated 25th Sept. 1961, is as follows:

> To Anne in remembrance of our book-hunting session and of last night when I laughed more than I can ever remember.
> Best wishes and good luck always from your book-mad friend,
> Mary

The writing is young and vigorous, that, I should say, of a woman in her mid-thirties or early forties (it is unlikely that anyone younger would have written such an inscription) – and therefore now, most likely, dead. Certainly I shall have been long dead when the same period of time shall have elapsed from now as between 'last night when I laughed more than I can ever remember' and now.

Of course, there are still many bibliomanes who insist that books should be in pristine condition, untouched by human pen, let alone by rings of coffee made by cups or mugs. An owner's inscription, unless he be famous enough to make the book an association copy, however neat, however cultivated the writing, is sure to make the book less valuable than it would otherwise have been – at least if it be less than a century old. This suggests that pristinists, if I may coin a word, are very numerous, more numerous indeed (or richer, perhaps) than people like me. And many collectors there are who are interested in books more for the arcana of their printing or their binding or some such auxiliary matter, and who go into ecstasies over the absence of a comma in line 27 of page 345 after the word *however* (clearly a printer's error), than in anything related even tangentially to their content. They remind me rather of those early enthusiasts for hi-fi equipment, who were so enamoured of the technical specifications of their equipment that they omitted to listen to anything on it. Or, to use Sir Karl Popper's famous metaphor about his opponent, Ludwig Wittgenstein, they are so busy polishing their spectacles that they never think to look through them.

Bibliomanes can indeed be very odd – odder even than I. The Reverend Charles Frognall Dibdin, in his famous but utterly unreadable book, *The Bibliomania; or, Book-Madness; Containing some Account of the History, Symptoms, and Cure of this Fatal Disease, in an Epistle Addressed to Richard Heber, Esq.*, which grew from a first edition in 1809 of 87 pages to a second two years later, in 1811, of 782 pages, probably the most rapid expansion of a subsequent edition of any book in the history of publishing (or in this case, self-publishing), and in itself a collateral symptom of 'this fatal disease.'

Dibdin's *The Bibliomania* was a response to a poem, also called *The Bibliomania, an Epistle Addressed to Richard Heber, Esq.*, by John Ferriar, MD. Ferriar was physician to the Manchester Infirmary; he was among the first to draw attention to the terrible living conditions of the industrial working class, and to link those conditions causally to the epidemic diseases to which they were prone. He wrote on other medical subjects such as hallucinations, but was also a literary scholar, for example editing the plays of Philip Massinger. His poem begins:

> What wild desires, what restless torments seize
>   The hapless man, who feels the book-disease…

And, indeed, one cannot help but feel that the Richard Heber, Esq, to whom both Ferriar's and Dibdin's epistles were address, was a hapless man. Independently wealthy, he roamed Europe in the search for rare volumes; rather unusually, he was keen on books printed in Mexico; by the time of his death, he had accumulated between 127,500 (Dibdin's estimate) and 160,000 volumes, stored in various places, including his five houses. His personal life was restricted by his passion for books, the aura of sexual impropriety hung over him, and his end was sad:

> He expired at Pimlico, in the midst of his rare property, *without a friend to close his eyes*, and from

all that I have heard I am led to believe he died broken-hearted: he had been ailing for some time, but took no care of himself, and seemed indeed to court death. Yet his ruling passion was strong to the last. The morning he died he wrote out some memoranda for Thorpe about books which he wished to be purchased for him.

His library (if that is what it should be described as having been) was sold after his death, and scattered to the four winds; it realised at sale the modern equivalent of £2,000,000 less than he had paid for it. As to whether it is better to die, as he did, still in the grip of an utterly futile quest, or to die calm of mind all passion spent

I find myself unable to decide. Do we need to blind ourselves to existential reality by means of our passion to the very end, or should we face the truth about our lives, unafraid and unillusioned? Whatever the answer, there is surely something very melancholy about so much enthusiasm, so much excitement, so much emotion, and no doubt so much erudition of a quirky kind, disappearing without trace – except, perhaps for the two epistles, themselves not known except to people a little like Richard Heber, Esq.

Dibdin, whose style was rococo, to say the least, drew comparatively short-winded attention in his first edition to some of the peculiarities of book collectors, to the bibliographical equivalent, in effect, of sexual perversions.

Among my favourites is the collector of *uncut* volumes, that is to say those volumes whose pages have to be cut by the purchaser in order to gain access to their contents. It is a curious fact of bookselling that an uncut volume is generally more expensive (and assuming the law of supply and demand) more desirable to purchasers than a cut equivalent. This is indeed strange; no purchaser of a car, for example, would prefer a vehicle without doors.

The preference for uncut, and therefore unreadable, volumes is not a new one by any means. I happened recently to be reading a slight volume of bibliomaniacal essays called *Books and Book Collectors* by John Carter, published in 1956. Carter was a distinguished bibliographer and bookseller, whose most important accomplishment, perhaps, was the exposure of the greatest British bibliophile and collector of his day, Thomas J Wise, as a forger and swindler who set up, printed and sold many supposedly rare volumes to his gullible customers, passing them off as hitherto unrecognised first editions. (They are, of course, now sought after in themselves, for a good forgery is worth its weight in gold, although never quite as much, of course, as if it were the genuine article. Why forgeries should be of lesser value, when they are recognisable as such only by the most minute analysis – Carter used chemical analysis of Wise's ink and paper, for example, in his exposure of him – is a question that is too remote from the supposed subject of this book, and if truth be told, too philosophically difficult, for me to tackle here.) Wise was not only a forger and a swindler, but a thief; he cut pages from rare volumes in the British Museum Library and reassembled them in very rare volumes of his own. He died a rich man, having started out a poor one.

Be that as it may, John Carter has an essay in the book I have mentioned called *Two Beckford Collections*. In it, he compares and contrasts two American bibliomanes (the distinction between -philia and -mania is fine one) whose 'subject' for collection was William Beckford, builder of Fonthill and author of the gothic novel, *Vathek*. No one, I think, would claim for him a very high place in the history of literature (incidentally, he wrote *Vathek* in French, not English), but two Americans, Mr Rowland Burdon-Muller and Mr James T. Babb, made every book, every document, by or related to him, the object of their acquisition. 'Beckford,' says Mr Carter, 'inspires a special devotion in those who collect him;' to which one is tempted to add, well, he would, wouldn't he?

The two collectors had slightly different approaches, however. Mr Babb was, if I may so put it, gourmand, while Mr Burdon-Muller was gourmet. The former would add anything of relevance to his collection, the latter insisted on the finest quality for items to gain admittance to his. Mr Carter says of Mr Burdon-Muller that:

> ... he has not allowed the absence of, say, a
> scrubby 1819 Paris reprint of *Vathek* to keep
> him awake at night, rare though it may be.

As evidence of the extremely high quality of the items in Mr Burdon-Muller's collection, we read:

> His first English *Vathek* (1786) in boards,
> uncut, is fine... His *Biographical Memoirs of*

> *Extraordinary Painters* (1780) Beckford's first
> book, is in the original marbled boards, calf
> back, uncut; his first Paris *Vathek* (1787) also
> uncut...

How vulgar and philistine it would be to cut the pages and
read the book! Poor Mr Burdon-Muller! One cannot help
but think of him as of a sexually-frustrated forty-seven-
year-old clerk in a municipal office who dreams of sexual
relations with the most famous model of his day. How
beautiful and fresh the print of the *Vathek* would be, if
only he could see it! Even if the scrubby Paris edition of
1819 did not keep him awake, I am sure the first English
Vathek (1786) and the first Paris *Vathek* (1787) did.

Vathek is a foolish book in a foolish genre; but people
will collect anything. I mention Messrs. Babb and Burdon-
Muller only to draw attention to the fact that, while I may
be strange in my relationship to books, there have been,
and no doubt are, many people stranger; I am, in fact, comparatively sane, in so far as I am not a collector of anything, more a mere accumulator, prepared however to pay
over the odds for a nice edition, or for a book that Mr
Carter elsewhere would call 'off-subject.' Since I have no
subject, all my books are in effect off-subject.

I cannot here forebear from quoting Mr Carter again, in
his essay on off-subject books. He illustrates what he
means by 'off-subject' by reference to collectors of the
works of Captain Mayne Reid, the nineteenth-century
writer of adventure books, such as *The Rifle Rangers* and *The
Scalp Hunters*. Reid also wrote, in 1860, a book on croquet,
very difficult to obtain for his collectors because of com-

petition from collectors of books about croquet.

Now anyone who has ever played croquet will know that, superficial appearances to the contrary notwithstanding, croquet is not so very different from scalp-hunting. It is, in fact, the best sublimation for human nastiness yet devised. But players of the game are as nothing compared with collectors of books about it, of whom Mr Carter says, they 'may not be numerous but will certainly be a grim and fanatical crew.'

28

False Economies

I must just relate the conversation I had on the subject of the value books with a young Dutch friend of mine, as I was driving him to the station (he missed his train). Writing a thesis on political philosophy, he was still young enough to be influenced in his views by others, including mine; he was not yet suffering from that condition almost universal among older intellectuals (such as I), namely a hardening of the concepts.

He had come by his own ratiocination to the conclusion that the cult of authenticity in art was wrong, bogus, and itself inauthentic. Why should a painting be twenty times as valuable if it is attributed to Rembrandt as it is if attributed to a member of his studio? After all, it is the same physical object, as beautiful (or not) in the one case as in the other; and, furthermore, it is now possible to duplicate endlessly works of art, so accurately that it takes effort to distinguish between them; why, then, should we so venerate the original? What does it matter – from the point of view of aesthetic judgment and therefore of value *sub specie aeternitatis* – whether the Versailles you visit is the one that Louis XIV actually trod, or a perfect replica built in China or Wyoming?

This is a young man's argument, of course, of the kind that I should once have loved. I was reminded of what Sir Leslie Stephen said in an essay on Swift, that young men think the world can be remade in a rational way, and judge rational what is in accord with their own beliefs.

But as it happens, the young man had also fallen in with a famous philosopher – a man far more eminent than I – who was proud of the fact that his very extensive library contained only cheap editions: because, he said, it is the content of books that counts, not anything extraneous about them such as the edition, binding, provenance, signature on the title page, etc. etc. And my young friend agreed with him.

Indeed, he had discussed the matter with his family, and had propounded with some warmth the view that nothing counted in a book but its contents. This was a matter of interest in his family, since, among other heirlooms, it was in possession of a first edition of Darwin (the *Origin of Species*, of course), and also of Malthus, whose views on population gave such an impetus to Darwin's thought. He was not interested in inheriting them, since they were no more to be valued than (shall we say) a cheap paperback version of the same books.

I said I thought this was a pity – for him – since a good copy of the Darwin sells for about £100,000, and the Malthus for several thousands. But in any case, I thought the matter needed slightly closer examination.

Let us, I suggested, perform a small thought experiment. Suppose a library possesses both a first edition of Darwin and a cheap paperback copy, and a fire breaks out in it. You have time to save one, but only one, of these copies; is it really a matter of complete indifference as to which you save? Surely very few people would say that it is not; and we should suspect those who said that it was either of not being quite true to their feelings, or of philistinism. But if it is accepted that the right thing to do in these circumstances would be to save the first edition, it follows that the two editions cannot be of precisely the same value, even if we think that the market price of the first edition is grossly or preposterously inflated.

It might be returned that the reason we choose to save the first edition is precisely because it is more valuable, as a mere matter of brute economic fact, whether we approve of it or not, and we should wish to preserve the economic value of contents of the library as much as we can. But this does not work either. For if we also suppose that the library is prevented by covenant from disposing of its books — not that any library these days feels bound by such things as covenants — the superior economic value of the first edition is of no use to it. In fact, it is not of superior economic value to the library, and might even be of less value, or at any rate more of a liability, in so far as the paperback version will take up less space, not need special protection etc., and would certainly be cheaper to replace if damaged. And yet still we would save the first edition in preference to the paperback.

This would suggest that the intrinsic worth of the two volumes is not at all the same, however inflated we may find the monetary value of one of them. And what is true of the first edition is also true of books that are signed, dedicated or once in the ownership of an historical figure. A book-rationalist might as well argue that a manuscript is not worth preserving because its content is more conveniently read in another form.

My young friend said that he was suspicious of the mania for signed or dedicated copies, or for those belonging to famous men, for the impurity of the motives behind it, an impurity that includes the element of financial speculation (monetary value is never more than few questions away in the minds of bibliomanes, as it is in the minds of collectors of other things, however refined they might otherwise pretend to be). He made an exception for books that had been dedicated to him personally, for clearly they had some direct connection to himself, with a corresponding power to evoke memories of the author. But this, I said, was not fully rational, either, according to his own style of argumentation; for surely if his memories were of any real significance to him they would remain without need of the *madeleine* of a signature.

The desire for mementoes is a civilised and civilising one. It is not only a recognition of the fleetingness of time, but of the importance of the past in the life of a man (using the word man in the broad, Addisonian sense). No doubt acquisitiveness of mementoes, relics and so forth can become pathological, but so can any other human tendency. The insistence on cheap modern editions at the expense of old on the grounds that the contents are exactly the same, and therefore they are of equal value, is to imply that our purposes of the present moment are all that counts in life: a sovereign means of depriving life of any possibility of transcendence.

29

Hair-Combing Pedants

Among the enemies of books not mentioned by William Blades in his *The Enemies of Books*, because it had not been invented when he wrote, is the ball-point pen. It is impossible to mark a book gracefully with such an instrument, and without destroying whatever beauty it might have as a physical object. No writing in ball-point pen will ever be beautiful however old it becomes: it is to calligraphy what concrete is to architecture, in that it cannot age well and will always be ugly. And I have noticed, in the manner of men noticing such things from the discontent of old age, that ever since the introduction and dissemination of this frightful invention the handwriting of almost everyone has deteriorated. You have only to compare the inscriptions of names in books pre- and post-1960 (say) to see that this is so. Whether the effort necessary to achieve a graceful hand is worthwhile in an age in which the ability to type is more important than the ability to write is another question entirely, of course. And this question is itself not very distant from the deepest questions of human existence: should we learn things only for their most utilitarian of utility, or for their own sake, and if the latter, for what proportion of our time in education?

Nevertheless, for the purposes of studying the markings in books, we must suppress our distaste for the form, in order to appreciate the content.

There are various genres of marking. One is that of the pedant, a genre that I hope it is not too pedantic to divide into two sub-genres. There is the pedant who in effect proof-reads books, keeping an eagle-eye out for misprints, and the pedant who pounces on errors of fact, such as a wrong date. Nowadays one would surely diagnose the former, who has much in common with the kind of bibliomane who finds his pleasure in the slight variations of editions, bindings and the like, as being mildly autistic or having Asperger's syndrome – because every human trait must find its medical diagnosis. Concerning oneself with trivialities is, of course, one means of keeping deeper anxieties at bay. As the Romanian peasant saying has it, the whole village is on fire but Grandmother wants to finish combing her hair.

A good example of the former type of pedant is the one who marked (in pencil, which in my youth I would have erased but now wish to preserve) misprints in my copy of Dr Ernest Jones' famous introduction to his edition of *Hamlet*: the one in which, surprise, surprise, he explained Hamlet's vacillation in killing Claudius by reference to his exceptionally severe case of Oedipal Complex. However, the truth or otherwise of this theory was not what moved the owner to mark the essay; it was the misprints, for example the missing *c* in the word can, in 'before it an be present to consciousness.' The missing letter appears demurely in the margin, as does the word *order* in the margin next to the line in which the words 'in other therefore' are printed.

Assuming that the marker was not the publisher contemplating a second edition, the man who did this was surely of a certain type. The misprints, after all, were not such as to render the meaning of the sentences opaque, and I was reminded of a geography teacher of mine, when I was eleven years old, who drew a triangle on the blackboard with his chalk. He then wrote the following words in it:

Paris

in the

the spring

and asked the class to write down what was written in the triangle.

He then asked all those who had written, as I had, 'Paris in the spring,' to put their hands up. A few others and I did so.

'You've got it wrong,' he said, and we were mortified briefly. (The teacher's name was Mr Dawson and he had a missing front tooth through which he lisped. It was only later, some time into my medical career, that I realised that missing front teeth were often symptomatic of drunken brawls.) Our mortification did not last long, however, for he quickly added, 'You are the more intelligent ones,' and explained how intelligence could lead to error. This was intended, perhaps, as a subtle initiation into the very necessary fact to be learnt that, where the human psyche was concerned, not all was straightforward or as it seemed. But it gave me a sense of pride from which I have never really recovered.

The pedant of the fact – pedantry's equivalent of the *noblesse d'epée* – is a marker of books too common to require illustrative example. His question and exclamation marks in the margins opposite an error come with almost audible snorts of delighted indignation (Professor Jackson, in her *Marginalia*, points out than no one ever puts more than five exclamation marks in a single row). He will happily correct in the body of the text a date that is out by a single day, or a statistic that, in his opinion, is out by a fraction. And this, of course, raises the interesting question of the pleasures of pedantry.

The pedant does not delight to find error because he is a lover of truth; he delights to find error to prove his superiority to whoever has made it. Love of power, therefore, has more in common with pedantry than love of truth; the pedant is a would-be dictator who dares not leave his library.

Honesty compels me to admit that I am far from immune from pedantry myself. I too have known the joys of nit-picking. For fourteen years I reviewed a book a fortnight for a well-known Sunday newspaper (until a new editor decided that the books pages needed more reviews by celebrities of books about celebrities written by celebrities, in accordance with our new democratic dispensation: government of celebrity, by celebrity, for celebrity). I had to control my natural tendency to apply, from sheer malice, the old legal maxim used to discredit witnesses, *falsus in uno, falsus in omnibus*: false in one thing, false in all. How delightful it is to catch out an expert or scholar in error (especially if it is gross) from one's own stock of common knowledge; and how easy to insinuate that, if he can make such an error, his whole life's work must be of little worth. This is a pleasurable indulgence in which, as in so many pleasures alas, must be rigorously controlled, if not outright suppressed: kept, like so many sexual fantasies, within the confines of the mind. And so I tried to control my tendency to make my reviews a list of errors that I had delighted to find, unless that is I thought them dishonest errors. Pedantry is a vice no easier, and no less necessary, to control than the others.

30

Magical Thinking

The commonest markings found in books are underlinings and lines down the outer margin of the text. In ballpoint pen they are peculiarly horrible, the equivalent of a scar across the cheek caused by a slash-wound. They emboss, but nastily, the other side of the page. The previous owner of my copy of John Stuart Mill's essay on Coleridge, a man who attended university in 1955 and whom I therefore will not name in case he should still be alive, changed halfway through his reading (and marking) from fountain to ballpoint pen. Perhaps this fixes the date at which fountain pens gave way to ballpoints; and the aesthetic effect was disastrous.

Even worse than scribblers with ballpoints are those who score through texts with marker-pens of luminous colour, usually a dilute yellow or a radioactive pink. I once watched on a German train, horrified, as a woman (cultivated, from the look of her) scored through the printed text of a book with a pink pen, line after line, page after page. First I wanted to tell her to stop it, but I have no German; then, before long, I wanted to strangle her. The book was a commonplace one of contemporary politics, but – to adapt the famous words of Heine slightly – those who deface books will sooner or later deface, or at least countenance the defacing of, much more.

The psychology of underlining is interesting. Many underliners seem rarely to get beyond the first chapter or two: underlining is generally more enthusiastic at the beginning than at the end of books. Perhaps this is because most books are far too long and have said all that they are going to say within the first two or three pages; or perhaps underlining is hard work and underliners have little mental or physical stamina or powers of concentration.

Like pedants, underliners come in two main types, those who underline a word, or a phrase at most, and those who underline whole passages. The former I understand, the latter not. The former method can be a useful aide-memoire, to bring attention to something specific for which one searches later, some time after one has finished the book. I now use this method myself, at least in cheap paperback editions, though in my youth and early adulthood it was hardly necessary for me, since I could go to the page and paragraph I needed – even quite a number of years later – after the most perfunctory search for it. I did not have a photographic memory as such, but a memory that functioned in some other way that allowed me to do this. Age, alas, has reduced this faculty.

But the purpose of underlining whole chunks of text eludes me. I think it is a form of magical thinking, akin to that of the reluctant student who carries his textbook with him everywhere he goes but never reads it, in the hope that its contents will somehow enter him as if books were embrocations for arthritis. I came across a particularly egregious example of underlining in chunks when I bought a book, Norman Sherry's *Conrad's Western World*, that had once belonged to the scholar of Conrad, Bruce E. Teets.

What little I know of the life of Professor Teets fills me with a deep, if only vague and ill-understood, sorrow. He was born in 1914 and died in 1997. He was a professor of literature at Central Washington University, and co-author of the 671-page *Joseph Conrad: an annotated bibliography of writings about him*, published in 1971 (the very year in which *Conrad's Western World* was published). I am sure he was intelligent, conscientious, diligent and extremely learned, but even I, with my taste for the arcane, cannot help but feel a sense of futility flood over me as I survey the title of his book. I recall Hazlitt's words about Shakespeare and those who have written about him (as, I confess, that I have done, in moments of weakness):

> If we wish to know the force of human genius, we should read Shakespeare. If we wish to see the insignificance of human learning, we may study his commentators.

Or, again, Doctor Johnson's:

> To adjust the minute events of literary history, is tedious and troublesome; it requires indeed no great force of understanding, but often depends upon enquiries which there is no opportunity of making...

Poor Professor Teets was not Conrad; he was not commenting on Conrad; he was not even commenting on the commentators on Conrad; he was merely listing the productions of the latter, an immense, indeed Herculean, labour, especially before the days of the internet: and while I am glad that the world is large and rich enough to support such abstruse erudition, I can hardly conceive that it was the fulfilment any man's dream to compile so obscure a work. Did not Professor Teets (who was born in West Virginia, as a brief search on the internet revealed to me) dream of being himself a great novelist in his youth? True, his name – anglicised German, I suspect – was against him; one can hardly imagine a great novelist, at least in English, called Teets; but he could have taken a pseudonym.

Professor Teets was a ferocious underliner, and in ballpoint pen. In all, he underlined on 136 pages, that is to say more than a third of the pages of the body of the work, and up to twenty lines at a time. He underlined perhaps an eighth of the text (no doubt he would have delighted to work out the precise percentage, as a means of keeping at bay night thoughts about the insignificance of human learning, at any rate his type of it). He can hardly have underlined so much as an *aide memoire*, or to fix the author's findings in his mind; I think, rather, that he was angry and frustrated. Such few words as he wrote in the margins were those of deep irritation: 'Why these three?' he asks petulantly of Professor Sherry's decision to use three of Conrad's books as a template for his biographical investigations.

I suspect (but am open to correction on the matter) that Professor Teets was angry that Professor Sherry's book and its predecessor, *Conrad's Eastern World*, were scholarly and of such intrinsic interest that a non-specialist could read them with pleasure and fascination. Indeed, they have remained in print more or less since they were published.

The anger of the underliner was directed at himself, for having achieved nothing comparable: he had only pedantry to fall back upon.

Of course, I might be entirely wrong; I am constructing a whole theory from a few ballpoint markings in a single book, and the title of another. But it is surely a fact that a life of learning is not necessarily a life of wisdom. The one requires qualities of intelligence and a minimum degree determination; the other far deeper qualities of character.

31

Self-Satisfacton

Among underliners, there is a sub-group who underline in more than one colour. Like other markers of books, they are inclined to underscore words that seem perfectly banal to people who are not party to their thoughts, which cannot be reconstructed by reference to their selections; but it is clear that red is always the colour of special emphasis.

In my possession is a book one of whose readers used three colours to underline, blue, green and red, like the flag of a newly-independent country. It is *The Crime of Punishment* by Dr Karl Menninger MD, published in 1968. It is inscribed by the author to Father René le Major, OP (Order of Preachers), Montreal, 'with kindest regards, Karl Menninger, MD.'

Am I alone, I wonder, in finding it odd, and not altogether attractive, that a man should sign his name followed by his degree? There is a self-satisfaction to it, or at least a determination not to be outdone in qualification by the addressee. It is one thing to address others using their qualification; it is another to refer to oneself in the same way. One senses (again, perhaps unjustly) that the MD is being used in advance support of the Bellman's great epistemological principle in *The Hunting of the Snark*:

What I tell you three times is true.

Of course, we all have our little vanities, the use of a title being one of them. The erstwhile President of Liberia, Samuel Doe, a man generally thought to have been semi-literate at the time of the coup that brought him to power, received an honorary doctorate from Seoul University in return for some logging concessions, and insisted on being called Dr Doe ever after. But it is not only African dictators who have this weakness. I have a letter from the writer, Anthony Burgess, written to an eminent professor, in which, apart from recommending his own books, he styles himself Dr Anthony Burgess – because of his honorary doctorates. And recently in Ireland friends told me that self-made Irish billionaires who were awarded honorary degrees insisted on being called 'Doctor,' though some of them did not even have their school leaving certifi- cate. I find these examples far less disagreeable, however, because more symptomatic of a normal human failing, than Dr Menninger's signature with its appended degree.

I didn't crack the code of the multicoloured underlinings. I don't even know whether they were those of Father le Major. When, for example, the following statement was underlined in green, did it indicate agreement, disagreement, or simply that it was believed to be important?

The law assumes men responsible and sane.

Whatever the underlining meant, Dr Menninger thought the law's assumption was unjustified and even vicious, for it led directly to punishment, which he regarded as a barbarous hangover of the mediaeval period. He was a great proponent of the following line of reasoning:

Men commit crimes because they are mentally ill.
We know that they are mentally ill because they
commit crimes.

This is a special example of the ancient idea than no man commits wrong knowingly. It boils down to the question of whether Man is good by nature, or whether he is a flawed being with a propensity to delight in evil. I find Dr Menninger's view of the matter unctuously self-satisfied, just as he would have found mine primitive.

The following passage, so redolent of his belief in his own superior level of understanding and compassion, was underlined in red: again, whether strong agreement or disagreement one cannot tell (though my guess is the former):

I suspect that all the crimes committed by all the jailed criminals do not equal in total social damage that of the crimes committed against them [by punishment].

All I can say is that Dr Menninger never had the advantage – the advantage from the point of view of grasping reality, that is – of living in today's Tower Hamlets or Moss Side. He strikes me as that rather typical figure of his era, the intellectual for whose generosity of sentiment someone else had to take the consequences.

Whatever the attitude of the underliner to Dr Menninger's opinions, he clearly grew tired of them, for his underlining stopped at page 42.

It was not the introduction of the ballpoint pen that brought about multicoloured underlining of books.

32

Self-Improvement

I once bought a marked book of no commercial value – not cheap, even at £2.50 – simply because the markings pleased and reassured me.

I bought it in the small market town where I live when I am in England. It is a lovely town, mentioned once in Shakespeare, but I hope its inhabitants will not take offence if I say that its literary culture, at any rate to judge from the books that one can buy in it, is neither deep nor wide. A harsh or censorious observer might put it even stronger.

However, in one of those charity shops that are now by far the most distinctive feature of British urban life, in that they are not found elsewhere in the world deemed civilised, I found, among the discarded novels of Danielle Steele and ghost-written autobiographies of minor television celebrities soon to be, if not already, forgotten, a copy of Palgrave's *Golden Treasury.*

The markings, in pencil, that moved me were conscientious annotations in a clear and almost childish (certainly not a sophisticated) hand, explaining either references to mythology, obsolete or obscure botanical terms, or words not already in the owner's vocabulary.

The book was printed in 1980, so that the markings must be recent, at least in the scale or within the span of my memory. I assume, then, that whoever marked it was considerably younger than I; and has studied English poetry with more seriousness, more devotion, more thoroughness, more desire for self-improvement, more tolerance of laborious enquiry, than I ever managed or, truth to tell, ever will manage. For example, when first I read the stanza in Thomas Gray's *Elegy in a Country Church-Yard* (a poem that, no doubt in disgracefully clichéed fashion, I think of always in a graveyard) that goes:

> Some village-Hampden, that with dauntless breast
> The little tyrant of his fields withstood,
> Some mute inglorious Milton here may rest,
> Some Cromwell, guiltless of his country's blood

I never pencilled neatly in the margin JOHN HAMPDEN MP 1594 – 1643, nor inserted a slip of paper as follows:

> John Hampden
> 1621 MP for Grampound later for Wendover later Buckinghamshire
> 1627 Imprisoned for refusing to pay share of a forced loan
> 1635 Refused again on the attempt to raise ship-money from inland places. Was prosecuted
> 1641 Party to the impeachment of Strafford
> 1642 One of the Members whose attempted arrest by the king led to the outbreak of the Civil War
> Raised a regiment of infantry – wounded at Chalgrove
> 1643 [accidentally written 1943] Died at Thame

The seriousness of the annotator's efforts at self-improvement is indicated by the willingness to annotate words that one might have expected one to know, for example the word *sophistry*, annotated as *the art of plausibly deceptive reasoning* (a good definition). Contrast this honesty with my own dishonesty in failing – no, refusing – to write the meaning of a word whose meaning I don't know in a cheap copy of a book in French or Spanish, though I know this method would help fix the knowledge in my mind, because I don't want anyone to see how deficient is my vocabulary in those languages. Pride struggles with desire for knowledge, and triumphs in the struggle.

The annotation of *sophistry*, incidentally, comes from a line in Ted Hughes' poem, *Hawk Roosting*:

> There I no sophistry in my body:
> My manners are tearing off heads –

I never entirely trust writers who use diminutives of their names. I doubt we would read Bill Thackeray or Betty Browning; and I find something mildly distasteful in Hughes' neopaganism, which seems to me redolent of a cross between a Nuremberg rally and a witch's coven held in a muddy field.

But to return to my annotator of Palgrave's updated *Golden Treasury*: I recognise something morally superior to myself, which is always good for the soul.

33

Room Furnishing

I am not a bibliomane in the sense of being one those people who are excited by the absence of a comma on page 247 of an otherwise commonplace book, though given a choice between the rare and the commonplace I choose the rare; but I am a bibliomane in the sense that Holbrook Jackson sometimes employs in his *Anatomy of Bibliomania* (the third edition of which, not coincidentally, is 852 closely-printed pages long, and so discursive that it makes the flight of my little essay seem arrow-straight by comparison): I suffer from that restless passion for books that if I am separated from them, shall we say for longer than three hours at the maximum, I begin seriously to fret and think that I am wasting my time. I will come back to this.

I am not so much a collector of books as an accumulator of them. In an odd analogy with the Malthusian law of population, I, like the eccentric bookseller whom I have mentioned, read arithmetically but buy books geometrically. However, I never buy one that I do not intend to read or refer to in some way, however distantly in the future (though now I have no distant future), and it is very curious how often a book is just the one I need twenty or even thirty years after I have bought it. Perhaps the internet will one day vitiate this pathetic pale excuse for my bibliomania, but that day has not yet arrived.

A person who accumulates a lot of books has somehow to arrange them. Of course, there are people who have books because they look good on shelves (as the title of Anthony Powell's novel has it, *Books Do Furnish a Room*, not a new thought, for Holbrook Jackson quotes Sydney Smith to the effect that 'no furniture is so charming as books, even if you never open them or read a single word,' a dictum that Holbrook says is often put into practice). I once wanted a book rebound by a binder so skilful that he deserves to be called an artist, who however could not oblige me until he had rebound an entire library of eighteenth-century books for a man who had recently become very rich indeed, and who bought cultural appurtenances by the kilo or the ton. And if I am honest, I have myself felt the temptation to range my books by their appearance on the shelf rather than by some other, slightly more scholarly principle, worthy of a so-called intellectual: a temptation that I have mostly resisted.

There is the Dewey Classification system, but what is appropriate to a huge public library serving untold numbers of people is not appropriate to a small and personal library, of whose contents the owner is mainly aware (though from time to time he will be surprised by a book that he has forgotten that he has), and who is likely to have the kind of memory that will, if he as arranged his library himself, allow him to lay his hand, give or take a yard or two of books, on the required volume.

If the Dewey is unnecessary (and of course disfiguring if its classification numbers are inscribed indelibly on to the spines of books), how does one arrange one's books? There can be very few people who have not dreamed of the 'right' or 'correct' way, that is to say the way of ordering their books in such a fashion that, once done, no further rearrangement will be necessary or even theoretically possible. They believe that, somewhere in the realm of Platonic forms, there is the perfect arrangement of their books, perfect from all points of view; and it is this Platonic form that they seek to reproduce in the sublunary world.

However, once the number of their books grows beyond some very small number, it soon dawns on them that their search is doomed to failure, and that, unless they want to be the bibliomanic equivalents of Sisyphus, they will have to make do with an arrangement that is good enough, which is to say tolerably convenient for their purposes. Of course, when their purposes change, as mine do regularly, they will find that the arrangement of their books will become less (rarely more) convenient than previously; but this is a cross that they have to bear, unless they are to be forever rearranging their books.

What is the subject matter of a book, and how does it relate to the subject matter of other books? Do I put *Madame Bovary* in arsenic, medicine and literature, or French literature (to mention only three of the sections of my library). Do I place *Bubonic Plague in Early Modern Russia* in my plague subsection of epidemic diseases (similar problems, of course, arise with Camus' *La Peste*, and a surprising number of other works of literature), or in the section of the history of Russia? When I put it in the one section, I immediately suffer from a nagging doubt that it really ought to be, or at any rate would be better, in the other. (I am thus like the Jewish mother who says, when her son puts on one of the two ties she had bought him for his birthday, 'What's the matter, don't you like the other one?') Of course, I could buy two copies, or however many necessary to have one in each relevant section, but buying two or more copies of *Bubonic Plague in Early Modern Russia* is mad, even by the pretty high standards of insanity of bibliomanes.

It very soon dawns upon a person with a substantial number of books that the possible or defensible ways of arranging them are practically infinite, and that therefore there is no 'right' way, if by right way is meant uniquely right, of doing it. But right and wrong are in this instance not symmetrical: for it does not follow that because there is no indubitably right, there can be no indubitably wrong way of doing things. In the absence of a perfect memory for the physical disposition of books, for example, complete randomness would be wrong: classification of some kind indubitably increases access to the books by, among other things, restricting the amount that has to be remembered by an overburdened mind. The same mistake is made by people who think that any prohibition whatsoever is a restriction on freedom, and therefore unwarrantable. Restriction is, in fact, essential to the practical exercise of freedom. Likewise, those who decry the teaching of grammar, on the ground that it restricts a child's possibilities of expression, mistake the nature of infinity, for it does not follow from the fact that certain things cannot be said that the number of things that can be said is not infinite. I am aware that this argument might give comfort to censors, who could use it to say that the prohibition of certain things is therefore no limitation of freedom of expression; but it seems to me that the objection to censorship lies somewhere else, if anywhere. (Besides, there is the undoubted historic fact that censorship, at least of a certain type, is good for literature and art in general, for all the greatest are and literature was produced under conditions of censorship. One has only to compare the literature of complete licence with that of qualified licence to know that this is so. And yet where are the public statues and memorial plaques to those unsung heroes of art and literature, to those who made great achievement possible, the censors?)

Each person in possession of books will range them differently, according to his own fancies and predilections. I know many people who, when they enter a house for the first time, are inclined (even if they control themselves) to go straight up to the bookshelves to find out what their hosts are made of: for taste is a more reliable guide to character than opinion. I am like this: I control myself, but in a room with a substantial number of books I feel a tension mounting in myself until I have found out what they are. Indeed, I often fake or manufacture a reason for sidling up to them, and examining them out of the corner of my eye. It is astonishing, when one has been around books a long time, how often one recognises a volume by some very tiny aspect of the appearance of its spine or dust wrapper.

Where there are a large number of books, a subtler indication of the owner's character can be discerned from their disposition: something that one has usually not the time to pursue. In the case of visitors to my library, this is perhaps just as well, for – superficially at least – what it tells them might alarm them.